C000151229

IMAGES
of England

WELLINGTON IN 1960

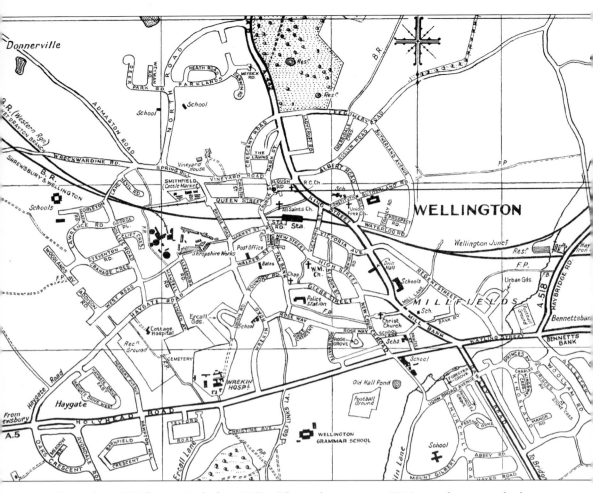

Town plan of Wellington in the late 1950s. The road structure in 1960 was almost exactly the same, although new streets and housing were being constructed between North Road and Admaston Road. The grounds of Apley Castle (top centre) marked the northern boundary of the town, hence the road names Parklands, Deer Park Road and Meyrick Road (Meyrick was the family name of the last owners of the castle). In 1960, long before the construction of the M54 motorway, the majority of the town lay between two major trunk roads: the A5 Holyhead-London Road and the A442 that provided the main north-south route. The railway line has bisected the town since it was laid in 1849.

IMAGES
of England

WELLINGTON
IN 1960

Allan Frost

Dedicated to my mother,
Mary Frost, a true Wellingtonian.

TEMPUS

View of central and northern Wellington, 1963. Copyright aerofilms.com.

First published 2002
Copyright © Allan Frost, 2002

Tempus Publishing Limited
The Mill, Brimscombe Port,
Stroud, Gloucestershire, GL5 2QG

ISBN 0 7524 2630 3

Typesetting and origination by
Tempus Publishing Limited
Printed in Great Britain by
Midway Colour Print, Wiltshire

Contents

Acknowledgements

Many people and organizations have contributed information and illustrations for this book, including Abbeycolor, J. Addison, E. Bagley, B. Bagnall, M. Baker, D. Bowyer, D. Briscoe, F. Brown, M. and P. Byram, R.S. Carpenter, G. Clayton, D. Cross, B. and M. Donaldson, E. Doody, H. Duckett, H. Caton, H. and D. Edwards, G. Evans, W. Fletcher, D. Frost, M. Frost, D. Gallear, M. Greatholder, J. Harris, P. Harrison, V. Harrison, K. Hitchin, V. and P. Hordley, D. Houlston, B. and M. Hullin, A. Kinder, C. Lane, J. Lewis, M. Machin, D. and V. Mann, W. Newbold, N. Pitchford, M. Price, R. Price, M. Purcell, A. and W. Rochelle, Shrewsbury Records and Research Library, *Shropshire Star*, *Telford Journal*, C. Treherne, D. Treherne, D. Trumper, R. and D. Vickers, E. and M. Wakeley, H. Wedge, Wellington Library and D. Whittingham.

I am very grateful to them all, as I am for the help and support given by my wife Dorothy, and I apologize sincerely to anyone who has been inadvertently omitted. No doubt they will let me know who they are!

Changed beyond recognition: the shops from above the top of the left-hand notice board to the corner of Victoria Street on the right in this stretch of New Street have all now disappeared. The author (seen here wearing his Park Junior School uniform at a wedding held at New Street Methodist church in 1960) is now just as unrecognizable.

Introduction

I am a Wellingtonian. A very proud Wellingtonian. I was born here and I grew up here. I have seen it change dramatically over the last fifty years (although the first few years are rather hazy), and not always for the better. My parents were born in Wellington; my grandparents ran a bakery and grocery shop in New Street. Even though I have lived in nearby Donnington and now Priorslee, my roots are still in Wellington and, I suppose, they always will be.

I have always been interested in my parents' earliest recollections of the town, which date from the years shortly before the First World War. What struck me during my childhood in the 1950s was that very little seemed to have changed except that motorized vehicles had almost completely replaced horse-drawn transport. In reality, of course, things had changed a lot. But not nearly so much as they have in the last forty years.

The Wellington of today is not the place in which I grew up. A good many folk considerably older than myself have witnessed greater changes over a period more than twice the length of

An aerial view of southern Wellington, c. 1958. Slums, including those in Parton (or New) Square had been cleared to the east of New Street Wesleyan Methodist church a few years earlier to make way for the proposed ring road, which was to be constructed in the early 1970s when Foundry Road and parts of Glebe Street and Tan Bank disappeared. The police station (the concrete building near the centre) opened in 1958, having moved from its previous restricted location on the corner of Church Street and Plough Road into new, purpose-built premises.

time on which I am able to comment. The 'old days' are invariably regarded with great affection; however, the reminiscences of older residents are often rather vague; they leave many questions unanswered. For example, folk remember specific shops as 'once belonging to' or 'used to be a', without giving any idea of a date. From a historical point of view, this can be very frustrating. Furthermore, memory tends to play tricks as time goes by; one decade can easily become merged with another. The result is that sequences of events get muddled. No one likes to admit that they could be wrong, and just because someone says or writes something doesn't necessarily mean it is right.

When I read an article in *Wellington News* (May 2001) about the discovery of photographs featuring Wellington in 1960, taken by Bernard Cross (a Shrewsbury photographer) and his employees, I knew they would provide the basis for a historically worthwhile book. Incidentally, copyright of the photographs is now owned by Abbeycolor of Shrewsbury – details on how reprints can be obtained through their agents in Wellington are given on page 128. The fact that the photographs were taken on a Sunday accounts for the virtual absence of people, and has the benefit of providing uncluttered views of streets and premises at that time. I have supplemented these with photographs and illustrations from my own research, reflecting the wide range of business and leisure activities.

I was ten years old in 1960. I already had some recollections of life in the town at that time and the photographs helped to revive some that had almost slipped away. Combining these photographs, all taken in or within a year or two of 1960, with facts and reports culled from a variety of contemporary sources (including, of course, the incomparable *Wellington Journal & Shrewsbury News*), I have tried to produce a snapshot of the town as historically accurate as possible. I have done my best to verify names, facts and details, and apologize in advance for any inaccuracies beyond my control.

I hope that this book, with its evocative illustrations, will rekindle memories among those of my generation and older, as well as showing younger readers and newcomers what Wellington was like before the pace of life quickened and Telford New Town was created. It is not intended to be a 'history' book as such, more of a trip down memory lane.

I hope you enjoy the views!

Allan Frost, July 2002

One

Setting the Scene

No town exists in a vacuum, however hard it tries. Every settlement is affected by events that take place around it. The degree to which those events affect the way a township develops, stagnates or withers depends on a wide range of factors. Frequently, towns are unable to decide their own destinies when forces beyond their control are exerted, or when the long-term effects of political decisions are underestimated. Townships become helpless victims when powerful vested interests and hidden agendas are brought into play. This is precisely what happened to Wellington in the late 1960s when discussions about a new town based on nearby Dawley ended and activity began to create the present reality of the Telford conurbation.

Despite considerable opposition, not only from Wellingtonians but also from other residents in the district (some of whom even refused to include 'Telford' in their postal addresses), the conurbation was imposed. Telford Development Corporation, granted staggering powers to ensure the success of this massive project, was regarded with as much hatred and disdain as the Romans must have been when they first set foot in this ancient Cornovian territory nineteen hundred years earlier. Indeed, the corporation's headquarters at Priorslee Hall were commonly referred to as the Kremlin, in much the same way as the Telford and Wrekin Council's Malinslee House is today by those who are highly sceptical of its motives, disenchanted by its actions and frustrated by the seemingly uncontrolled power it wields.

Wellington has struggled to come to terms with a loss of status brought about by the ill-considered decisions of people with little or no regard for the social history of the area, who seem to excel at spending considerable sums of money destroying any real sense of social cohesion and community spirit.

It was not like that in 1960 when Wellington was a thriving market town, the main centre for shopping, services and entertainment in this historically rich area of east Shropshire. Like many English towns at that time, it sought to improve its public amenities and the quality of its council housing. For some 150 years Wellington had grown in stature, and was rightly regarded as the prime commercial centre in an area of important industrial development. People from surrounding villages and towns flocked here to buy the necessities of life and enjoy its wide variety of cultural and sporting activities. Wellingtonians seldom needed to travel out of the town; virtually everything they needed was present on their doorstep.

In many ways, Wellington's location on the edge of the east Shropshire coalfield was fortuitous. It did not suffer the same extreme economic up- and downturns experienced by Donnington, Madeley or Coalbrookdale, where acres of land became derelict from the late nineteenth century onwards. Wellington was able to benefit from its own main-line railway depot and the arterial roads that cross at the Cock Hotel. Whereas larger concerns like Joseph Sankey & Sons, Sinclair Iron Works, Granville Colliery and the Central Ordnance Depot provided employment for thousands of workers, Wellington comprised countless small businesses catering for the everyday needs of ordinary folk; it did not rely on any single product or service to sustain itself. Furthermore, it was a centre for the farming community as well as for an increasingly urbanized population. It was, in short, an extremely diverse commercial centre.

Just how small some of the businesses were is evident when photographs of their premises in this book are compared to those existing today. Some have since been demolished as part of Wellington Urban District Council's housing strategy during the 1960s, as happened to much of Glebe Street, High Street and parts of New Street. Others have been amalgamated with adjacent premises to create the larger shops so favoured by the national chain stores whose presence has been actively encouraged by the planning authorities.

The demise of these smaller traders, many of whom lived above their shops, together with remarkable increases in the annual business rates charged by successive councils, undoubtedly led to Wellington becoming a shadow of its former self during the 1980s and 1990s. 'Footfall', the trite name given to denote the number of people visiting a shopping area, fell dramatically at that time but is now improving, as more people come to realize that it is less stressful to shop in a 'proper' market town than in an out-of-town precinct where parking is difficult, service is often indifferent and unjustifiable prices are frequently charged for a comparatively limited selection of goods.

The Wellington of 1960 was entirely different. Parking was rarely a problem because most people didn't have motor cars; bikes and buses were the most common forms of transport. The

Work begins building new blocks of flats and maisonettes in High Street. An immense amount of demolition work took place, ostensibly to rid the town of unsightly slums. Jack Beard's tripe-dressing shop is on the extreme right, adjacent to Lawson Miller Bowman's barbers shop. Mr Bowman acquired the business from its previous owner Ben Robertson around 1941 and died in 1960; the premises were subsequently demolished. Copyright Abbeycolor.

streets and shops were packed with people who weren't in so much of a rush. Groups congregated on street corners, and especially in Market Square. Gossiping over a coffee in one of the town's cafes was part of the Saturday routine, just as Mondays were always washdays.

Residents of provincial towns are seldom greatly influenced by national or international affairs unless their own lives are affected, as happened in Wellington during the two World Wars and, to a lesser extent, the Suez Crisis of 1956. The standard of living for those who had survived the Second World War improved immeasurably during the 1950s, yet the threat of another world conflict was ever present. The perceived threat of the Bomb, the Cold War with the USSR and the latter's support for Iraq, the invasion of Panama by Cuba's Fidel Castro, President Kruschev's visit to communist China, unrest in parts of Africa (especially Kenya, Southern Rhodesia, South Africa and the Congo) and American activities in Indonesia caused some concern to locals during 1959, but not nearly so much as a shortage of fish because of the 'cod wars' with Iceland during which gunboats protected the British fishing fleet.

Such events were followed with a semi-detached interest; no one believed the apocalyptic terrors of the Second World War would ever be allowed to recur. And as for the United Nations condemning apartheid and racism, well, that wasn't anything to do with Wellington. Yet. The influx of migrants from the West Indies and the Indian sub-continent was only just beginning. The closest most indigenous Wellingtonians had been to foreign immigrants was at Mann's Chinese laundry in High Street.

But things were beginning to change. People appreciated having spare cash in their pockets and were prepared to spend more on luxury goods (like televisions) and leisure activities.

Although they didn't know it, many long-established family businesses were on the verge of closure. Some were able to adapt and would survive, for a while at least.

Market Square looking north towards Church Street. Note the absence of road markings. Copyright Abbeycolor.

A 1960-61 Wellington Urban District Council meeting in the Walker Street Council Chamber. Pictured, clockwise from the left, are: -?-, Philip Bott, Joe Pearce, Hubert Case, Bill Fisher-Jones, John Lovatt, George Evans, Graham Murphy, Sidney Parker, John Addison (chief public health officer), Tom Edwards, Alan Myatt (deputy financial officer), Alan Hartland, Dan Draper (deputy engineer and surveyor), Fred Parkinson (deputy town clerk), Miss Edwards (committee secretary), Dr Stuart, Reuben Rushton (town clerk), Agnes Jones (chair), Father Abbey (chaplain and vicar of Christ Church), Arthur Barten (engineer and surveyor), Oliver Leighton (chief financial officer).

Wellington Rural District Council offices in Tan Bank, with a patriotic Union Jack flag flying.

Two

Official Bodies

Ever since its inception in 1894, the Wellington Urban District Council had taken its duties to improve amenities and housing very seriously. Over the course of its existence the social background of councillors had undergone gradual change, so that by 1960 traditional landowning gentry with a supposed paternalistic interest in the welfare of the town and its inhabitants had been supplanted by businessmen, 'professionals' and 'ordinary' folk.

It is not within the sphere of this book to comment on the reasons why people choose to put themselves forward for election as council members but, then as now, there was a general belief that representatives could be trusted to put the town's interests before their own. The fact that these representatives were Wellingtonians to the core inevitably led to some blinkered decisions, much to the frustration of relative newcomers, but it has to be acknowledged that they represented most of the population who had also grown up in the town and understood its origins and aspirations.

Important decisions had already been taken to introduce new housing. The council-owned estates on both sides of Dawley Road had been completed, and some slums to the east of New Street Methodist church had been demolished some years earlier to make way for the proposed ring road. Attention was now being turned to two areas considered ripe for development: one

Wellington Urban District Council Chambers building, Walker Street. Copyright Abbeycolor.

The Nelson Inn at No. 36 High Street. The last licensee was Jean Webber. Copyright Abbeycolor.

High Street, looking towards New Street. On the left-hand side are, from left to right: Mrs Clarke's home and lodging-house, followed by William Morris's former butchers shop and the sign of The Nelson Inn. The Three Crowns inn sign is visible on the right-hand side of the road above the distant parked car. New premises for Avery Scales and Shropshire Fireplaces are being built centre right, where a group of cottages, including Corbett's Yard, previously stood. The Duke's Head (known as 'The Bottles') pub is just beyond them. Between the building work and the soldier are Clifford's hairdressers, Jervis's café, Austin's newsagents and Mann's Chinese laundry. Copyright Abbeycolor.

was former farm- and parkland to the north west of North Road; the other was an area of run-down properties bounded by High Street, Glebe Street and St John Street. New houses were built privately off North Road from 1958 onwards and considerably more, including flats and a new secondary school at Dothill, were scheduled; the development off North Road was considered vital to attracting younger people and their families to the town.

Compulsory purchase notices served on properties around High Street in 1956 caused a public outcry, most particularly from Rollason's scrap merchants and Frost's the bakers, because the council had made no provision for these businesses to be relocated and the timing (just before Christmas) indicated a callous disregard for the feelings of long-established and well-respected townsfolk. After several appeals the council allocated land for a new tip for Rollason's off Haybridge Road (although their business continues to operate in High Street opposite the site of their old tip) and the Frost family retained their premises at the top of New Street until 1970 when Ernest Frost, the last of the family to own the shop, retired. The Chad Valley toy factory, also at the top of New Street, was omitted from the plans because it was a flourishing enterprise and had too many workers; the council could not afford to pay so much compensation or be seen to put so many employees out of work.

The character of the large tract of land between High Street and Glebe Street acquired by the council altered completely from 1960 onwards. After Rollason's scrap yard had been cleared (much to the annoyance of boys who found its contents a treasure trove when making go-carts), everything else was demolished to make way for blandly-designed, functional flats and maisonettes intended for occupation by council tenants. Soon the small cottages, many with dirt floors and limited sanitation, the Glebe and Nelson public houses, Clarke's lodging house and sundry shops had disappeared, and all their occupants were relocated. An old area of Wellington, regarded by its inhabitants almost as a town in its own right, had gone forever.

Member of Parliament for the Wrekin constituency in 1960 was Bill Yates (Conservative). Despite his best endeavours for many years, Mellor Harrison, the Labour agent in Wellington, would have to wait until 1965 for the area to return a Labour MP, lecturer Gerry Fowler.

Valeting Service laundry, 2 High Street, then scheduled for demolition. The entrance to St John Street, named after St John Chiverton Charlton, Lord of Apley Castle, is on the right. Copyright Abbeycolor.

On opposite sides in the world of politics. Left: the highly regarded and much liked Labour agent Mellor Harrison. Born in 1911 at King's Cross, Halifax, he came to this area in 1944. He died in 1981. Right: Bill Yates, Conservative Member of Parliament for the Wrekin constituency.

The flat-roofed Ministry of Labour dole office in Tan Bank, where claimants were required to report daily, stands beyond the Halifax Building Society (formerly the Tan Bank café) and Bill Pollard's hairdressing and sweet shop. Chetwood's garage (now a car park) is next door and the Primitive Methodist schoolroom and chapel are at the far left end of the road. The 'Snacks' sign marks the entrance to the billiards hall. Copyright Abbeycolor.

Of the two men, Mellor was probably the best-liked. Bill, while certainly a most conscientious and competent MP who, during 1960, was involved in government discussions concerning draft proposals for the creation of a new town centred on Dawley to relieve housing problems in the Birmingham conurbation, failed to appreciate the rapid change in social attitudes developing at that time. Mellor, on the other hand, was much more down to earth. Even if his views weren't shared by everyone, his straight talk and considered manner gained him much support and many friends, and not just among traditional working-class supporters.

The police had occupied their new purpose-built station at Glebe Street since 1955, having moved from rather cramped accommodation on the corner of Church Street and Plough Road. The fire brigade, for many years located in Foundry Road, had moved to purpose-built premises in Haybridge Road in 1956. The Cottage Hospital in Haygate Road, gifted to the town by John Crump Bowring in 1912, continued to provide a valuable service, as did the Wrekin Hospital on Holyhead Road. Children's welfare was catered for in a small clinic, also in Haygate Road.

Two hospitals served the needs of most patients. Wrekin Hospital (a former workhouse) treated general accidents and fairly minor ailments (particularly of the elderly) and had an excellent maternity unit. The Cottage Hospital also patched up many people with minor injuries (the author once received stitches for a finger wound. Unfortunately, the nurse wasn't so attentive when the stitches were removed and couldn't understand why the thread wasn't coming out as she pulled it. It took a few agonizing moments before she realized she was pulling the wrong end of the thread and that she'd been trying to tug the knot through the skin). People with more serious ailments and injuries were treated in the Royal Salop Infirmary at Shrewsbury.

There was no single doctor's surgery in the town in 1960: general practitioners operated from several premises. Wellington's doctors then were H.W. Bambridge, D. Hewatt-Jaboor and W.R. Pooler at The Villa, Church Street; I.E. Davidson at Crescent House, Whitchurch Road; George Pollock and P.M. Wormald at the bungalow in Victoria Avenue; J. Redfern at Park Walls and Winifred Malet at 22 Mill Bank. Patients in waiting rooms would sit, quietly reading well-thumbed out of date magazines and comics, while clutching metal tokens embossed with numbers signifying their place in the queue.

National Assistance and County Court offices in Walker Street. Copyright Abbeycolor.

The annexe to the tax office at Belmont Hall. The rough ground in front was a car park used in early December by a travelling fair.

The tax office cricket team. From left to right, back row: Lawrence Wright, Frank Whittall, Stuart Geldhill, Jack Rothwell, Dave Price, Max Turner (umpire). Front: Pat Clare, Nigel Pitchford, Ewart Duckfield, Guy Lawton, Max Freeman (district inspector).

National Health Service dentists were L.R. Bradford at 'Springville', Vineyard Road; J.E.C. Dickin at Queen Street Chambers and F.E. Pratt at 58 King Street. Wellington also boasted two private chiropodists: Colin Evans at 1 Market Street and Sidney Hughes at 7 Mill Bank.

Children who were unfortunate enough to be neglected by their families or who had behavioural problems were accommodated for varying periods of time at special establishments: The Vineyard in Vineyard Road; The Mount at the corner of Wrekin and Haygate Roads; and Flora Dugdale's Girls Home in Wrockwardine Road.

Unemployed adults registered at and received meagre benefits from the Labour Exchange in Tan Bank; the National Assistance office was in Walker Street, as were the offices of the County Court. HM Inspector of Taxes occupied Belmont Hall, a rambling Victorian building that had been a private grammar school, located behind The Majestic ballroom (the rooms above which constituted the Tax Office in the 1930s). The Tax Office had expanded into a small annexe to Belmont Hall during the 1950s. Waste ground in front of the Hall was used as a car park (as was the vacant land east of New Street Methodist church) and occasionally for travelling circuses and the funfair held each year in early December. Previously the fair had often been held in Haybridge Road on land that had been acquired for building the Walker Technical College.

There are three aspects of the town which deserve special mention. The first is the swimming baths which were reasonably well maintained and a great source of fun, not just to members of its own swimming club and the general public, but also to hoards of screaming children who frequented it as part of their school physical education classes. The second is the care and attention given to the maintenance of the Bowring Recreation Ground off Haygate Road and the gardens of All Saints Parish church; they were a great source of pride, always a pleasure to see. The third is the cleaning of the town's streets; there was very little litter and no graffiti to speak of. Residents cared a great deal about the appearance of the town.

Left: the general post office in Walker Street with old-fashioned telephone boxes outside and the Urban District Council chambers beyond. Right: the children's library, at this time occupying its own premises away from the main library, further along Walker Street. The building now constitutes part of Gwynne's solicitors. Both photographs copyright Abbeycolor.

The Westminster Abbey train waits to depart for Wolverhampton from the 'up' line platform, with All Saints parish church in the background. Before the 1963 Beeching Plan cuts in services, Wellington station was a busy junction, with several bays in addition to three main platforms. Copyright R.K. Blencowe.

Engine sheds at Wellington. The sheds were used to carry out maintenance operations and housed several pannier engines. These panniers were used, among other functions, to haul freight trains to and from factories in the surrounding area. Copyright R.S. Carpenter.

Three

Transport

One measure of a town's importance is how well it is served by public transport and the capacity of its car parks. The main car parks in Wellington at this time were The Parade and the waste land on both sides of New Street Methodist church. Others could be found at Ten Tree Croft and Foundry Road. Parking was also permitted at certain times (although road markings were few and far between) in Market Square and along streets leading into the town centre. Although car ownership was becoming more commonplace, the majority of people still did not own any form of motorized transport.

Wellington railway station provided a vital and regular service to many other towns and villages in or near the east Shropshire coalfield, including Hadley, Trench, Donnington, Ketley, Oakengates, Dawley, Horsehay, Madeley, Ironbridge and Much Wenlock. The branch lines serving these communities were well supported by passengers, and by businesses that used them to carry substantial quantities of raw materials from the mines and finished goods from the factories. There were also frequent loads of low-grade coal taken to the Ironbridge electricity power station near Buildwas. All of these branch lines were destined for closure under Dr Beeching's ill-considered axe blows from 1963 onwards.

There were also popular main-line services to Shrewsbury (then referred to as 'Salop' by locals), Market Drayton, Stafford, Wolverhampton and beyond. British Railways often put on excursion trains to exotic venues like Barmouth and York during the summer months, and it was quite common for organized groups such as the scouts to charter trains for special trips, in

Railway footplate men relaxing in the Station Hotel. From left to right: drivers Joe Burden and Bill Bennett, firemen Arthur Mannering and Jack Hicks, locomotive shed master Frank Sumner.

much the same way as buses could be hired. Wellington station always seemed to be busy, delays not too frequent and with clean refreshments and waiting rooms.

Bus services provided greater flexibility and more frequent travel than the railways; they had the added advantage of being able to stop almost anywhere between centres of population, however small. The downside was that space was limited, particularly on market days (then Thusdays and Saturdays) when everyone had to cram themselves, countless shopping bags and baskets as well as a few pushchairs and the occasional dog (invariably the size of an alsatian) into an inadequate space. With tyres and axles groaning under the strain, the buses crawled along the pot-holed surfaces of narrow roads and lanes. Sometimes it was necessary for several passengers to alight to help buses struggle up not-so-steep hills.

These services were provided by the Midland Red Omnibus Company, which tended to operate from Queen Street, and members of the Shropshire Omnibus Association, a loose alliance of privately-owned bus companies whose terminus was in Victoria Street. The Midland Red catered well for passengers wishing to travel longer distances (to Shrewsbury, Wolverhampton and Birmingham), although it did also operate routes in the town and outlying district, whereas the Association concentrated on the townships around what is now regarded as Telford and nearby villages like High Ercall. Friction often occurred, not just between Midland Red and Association drivers but also between Association members themselves, especially where routes shared a common road or junction. The most frequent accusation was of poaching, where drivers would delay their departure time or drive slowly along the route and pick up people who intended to catch the bus following theirs.

The Victoria Street bridge over the railway line was so narrow that buses operated a one-way system (although it didn't apply to private vehicles) down High and New Streets into Victoria Street and forward into King Street. The amount of traffic congestion on market days, especially Saturdays, had to be seen to be believed. The number of people wanting to shop or visit the cinemas or football ground in Wellington was immense, to say the least. To cope with demand, double the number of normal-service buses was provided for most of the day. Some

Midland Red booking office and bus stands in Queen Street. Jay's café provided refreshments for waiting passengers who, if they looked at the posterboard resting on the ground, would see that The King and I *was again showing at the Clifton cinema due to popular request. Copyright Abbeycolor.*

22

Victoria Street bus terminus with the Co-op pram shop on the left and Gordon Lee's bike shop on the right. The Naish family lived in one of the houses beyond Lee's. Victoria Motor Co.'s car repair yard is opposite the bus and before the narrow turning into waste land behind houses in Victoria Avenue. Wheeler's pet shop grain storerooms are to the left of the bus stands. The bridge over the railway not only had an awkward bend immediately before it but was also very narrow; it had, after all, been constructed at a time when horse-drawn carts prevailed. From the Second World War, bus drivers observed a voluntary one-way system to reduce the number of hold-ups and frayed tempers. Other road users were not affected. Cottages in King Street, now long gone, can be seen beyond the bridge. Copyright Abbeycolor.

John Jervis's bus fleet at the garage off Regent Street, near the Tin Bridge over the railway line.

routes (such as to Hadley, Trench and Donnington) had buses leaving every five minutes, and they would be so packed that conductresses struggled to collect fares and issue tickets. The termini were also very busy at about eleven o'clock on Saturday nights, when revellers, cinema- and dance-goers caught the last buses home. It could be a long walk or an expensive Brown's taxi ride if they were too late... and girls particularly would have some explaining to do to their parents.

Like the Midland Red, the Association ran 'specials', such as to the foot of the Wrekin Hill on Easter and Whit Mondays (for walkers wishing to climb the hill or ride on the swing boats at the Halfway House where refreshments were served), trips to Eyton Races, theatre and shopping trips to Birmingham and London, seaside excursions and, of course, services to and from football matches.

The increasing popularity and relative affordability of motor cars (an Austin A40 cost £465 plus £194 purchase tax whereas a Humber Super Snipe would set the purchaser back £1050 plus £438 purchase tax) not only meant greater flexibility of travel, it also gave a powerful impetus to the increasing numbers of garages required to service those cars (as did the annual MOT inspection on cars over ten years old, imposed from 12 September 1960) and fill them with petrol. Some garages also repaired motor cycles and scooters – Bill Doran and Matt Wright's in Park Street Garage and Harry Stanford's at 99 King Street were considered the best in this field.

There was always the humble bicycle for those who wished to avoid public transport, the expense of a car and sore feet. Several shops catered for their needs, including repairs, most notably Bill Perry in Church Street, Harry Sutch at the Cock Hotel crossroads and Gordon Lee's in Victoria Street. Curry's in New Street (where Gordon had previously been manager) always had an excellent range of new bikes.

A few children enjoyed the dangers of 'driving' home-made go-carts lovingly nailed, bolted and screwed together from oddments retrieved from Rollason's tip; New Hall Road and Chapel Lane were popular race tracks (Chapel Lane, despite its rough and uneven surface, was the best in-town toboggan run during freezing winter weather). Someone had to keep a watchful eye out for traffic and, of course, for policemen walking the beat. Other children hurtled along on roller skates or foot scooters.

Chetwoods Garage service department opposite the main showroom and offices in Tan Bank. Copyright Abbeycolor.

FOR A NEW
**AUSTIN
FORD
JAGUAR**
★ ★ ★

| GUARANTEED USED VEHICLES ALWAYS ON OFFER | SERVICE and REPAIRS BY WORKS-TRAINED MECHANICS | COMPLETE RANGE GENUINE AUSTIN AND FORD SPARES IN STOCK | MODERN GREASING BAY. WHILE-YOU-WAIT FOAM CAR WASHING ETC. |

THE WAVERLEY GARAGE (WELLINGTON) LTD.
PHONES 671-2

Contemporary advertisement for the Waverley Garage, Church Street, where cars were both sold and maintained. The showroom window also displays miniature, fully-working cars for the children of people well enough off to own private land on which the cars could be driven: driving them on the public highway was illegal.

E. Brown & Son's taxis were located between The Majestic ballroom and the rough road leading to Belmont Hall. On the other side of the road was the wooden hut where the Darby and Joan club met; it had previously been used as a canteen for workers at the Chad Valley toy factory. Copyright Abbeycolor.

Curry's double-fronted cycle and radio store at 45 New Street. Curry's also sold a tempting variety of, including Triang cars, go-carts and prams as well as Dinky, Matchbox and Corgi vehicles. Rose & Co.'s wallpaper and paint shop is to the left and R. Minton's hairdressers is to the right. One of the most noticeable aspects of men's and ladies' hairdressing salons during 1960 was that they all seemed to have a wide range of branded cigarettes on sale as well as the usual array of hair care products like Brylcreem (for dashing male clients) and lacquer sprays (ostensibly for the women). Barber's shops sold 'something for the weekend, sir?' discreetly to outwardly macho, inwardly embarrassed, hopefuls. Copyright Abbeycolor.

Bill Perry's bicycle sales and repair shop in Park Street. The workshops were on the left while living accommodation was on the right. The council tried to have the buildings demolished but, tastefully renovated, they still remain.

Four
Food Stores

As with any market town, Wellington had a large number of shops selling fresh meat and vegetables, supplied, in the main, by neighbouring farms. A livestock market was held at The Smithfield off Bridge and Vineyard Roads on Mondays; many men, including farm hands, took advantage of the fact that some public houses, especially The Smithfield, extended lunchtime drinking until well into the afternoon.

The public market was held on Thursdays and Saturdays in the Market Hall and must be considered one of the best in the country at that time. It sold an enormous range of products. Several shops in the town also rented stalls in the market, partly to raise their profile to the buying public but also to cope with the increased demand for foodstuffs on market days when the shops themselves simply couldn't cope. Customers came equipped with string bags and wicker baskets; plastic bags had yet to replace thick paper carrier bags.

As befits a market town, there were several butchers (at least fourteen), some specializing in pork: Espleys, for example, had three sets of premises in New Street, the main one of which slaughtered pigs and processed the meat into pork pies and various cuts. Owens's in High Street also slaughtered pigs on its premises. Other butchers dealt with beef and lamb, or poultry. Fresh

The gates to Espley's slaughter yard (on the extreme left) were located next to George Dunn's confectionery shop at No. 3 Tan Bank. The property on the right had once been J.R. Dickinson's tailor's shop; he had died in 1943. Copyright Abbeycolor.

fish could be bought from Smith's at 65 New Street or from Mac Fisheries at 10 New Street. Smith's was a traditional fishmonger's, where fresh and smoked fish of all types, arranged in rows, stared wide-eyed but lifeless from their marble slabs. Mac Fisheries was a more modern concern with clinical white trays laid out in refrigerated cabinets. The unmistakable whiff that only fresh fish can emanate pervaded both stores and the air immediately outside.

The majority of food stores in Wellington were small, family-run businesses; many of the proprietors lived above or behind their shops. Some had quite a thriving trade, while others just about managed to eke out a precarious profit. There were already some multi-purpose stores and signs of takeovers by national companies. Although supermarkets as such did not exist here in 1960, a few stores that offered a wider choice were beginning to attract larger numbers of customers, who collected their provisions in wire baskets on their way to the till; trolleys (and wider aisles) had yet to be introduced. Not only were these stores, like Melias in Crown Street and New Street and Lloyds in Market Square, able to buy in bulk, they were adjusting their product lines to take advantage of the increasing use of refrigerators in ordinary homes. People no longer needed to buy fresh food, such as dairy produce, meat and vegetables, on a daily basis. Housewives were slowly becoming liberated from at least a few traditional chores.

Most milk supplies were delivered door-to-door by one of the town's dairies (these included Meredith's Red House Dairy on Holyhead Road and Arleston Dairy) or independent milkmen, like Fred Treherne. Orange juice, bread, eggs and occasionally fizzy pop and cordials were also delivered from the milk van. Milk, of course, was delivered in pint glass bottles. Milk in cartons was the sole province of roadside vending machines that never worked when you needed them to. (Actually, Sankey vending machines could deliver the goods without payment if the right part of the machine was thumped hard and the dispensing mechanism dislodged.)

Taking everything into consideration, Wellington was an excellent place to buy food in all its forms. The quality was good and it was guaranteed to be fresh.

Market Street, looking towards the Square Café in Market Square. Market Hall, with its peripheral shops, is on the right-hand-side of the picture. Behind the solitary pedestrian on the left is Norman Jellyman's gents' and boys' outfitters; Norman moved here because his former premises at No. 4 New Street were demolished early in 1960. Copyright Abbeycolor.

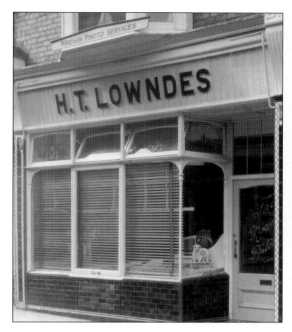

Family butchers Lowndes (left) and Onions, both in New Street. Wrekin Photo Services operated from above Lowndes's shop at this time. Both photographs copyright Abbeycolor.

Mason Bros ham and bacon shop on the corner of Duke Street. Don Duffett's paint and wallpaper store, on the left, ran through the building from Duke Street into Crown Street. Valeting Services had recently moved their laundry business from the empty property on the corner of Crown Street (seen here on the right) to Church Street; they also had premises at No. 2 High Street, which would be demolished around 1966. Copyright Abbeycolor.

J.C. Lloyd & Son's 'high class provisions' store at 17 Market Square. It was common practice to lower blinds overnight and at weekends to ensure product packaging did not fade in the sun. Some blinds were made of tinted, see-through, thick plastic sheets, which enabled passers-by to view the goods inside. Copyright Abbeycolor.

Melias grocery shop in New Street. Espley's pork butchers was next door and can just be seen on the extreme right of the picture. Butter and lamb prices during 1960 fell because of increased imports from New Zealand and Australia. The narrow archway between the two shops led to Espley's food-processing plant and the slaughter yard at the rear. Copyright Abbeycolor.

One of several Oakengates & District Co-operative Society stores in the town, this one selling groceries at 44 New Street, where regular customers were encouraged to call again to collect redeemable dividend stamps. The Co-op claimed to offer reduced prices because it owned many of its supply companies. Copyright Abbeycolor.

Ison's grocery store at 16 New Street with Dewhurst family butchers at number 18. Ison's adopted the system of advertising prices in the shop window so that shoppers could compare their prices with those of their rivals; smaller, traditional 'corner' shops didn't go in for that sort of thing because they were not able to benefit from bulk buying. Copyright Abbeycolor.

Mac Fisheries at 10 New Street, sandwiched between Preedy's tobacconists and Myladi's women's outer- and underwear shop, the latter of great fascination to juveniles who stood in intrigued wonderment until a clout put an end to their reveries. Copyright Abbeycolor.

Jones's electrical store in New Street followed by Waterworth's greengrocers, Cotton's ironmongery, Quality Cleaners, Bean's gents' outfitters and Daffern's drapers and milliners shops. Mr E.W. 'Skipper' Jones, a former chairman of Wellington Town Football Club, also had a store in Market Square. He died in October 1960. Copyright Abbeycolor.

Nos 57 to 65 New Street (from left to right), with Smith's art and needlework shop, Kearton's outfitters, Wheeler's pet supplies and Smith's fishmonger's (established in 1850). The fishmonger's closed during 1960 and the premises became the Ming Fung – the first Chinese restaurant in the town – by December of that year. Copyright Abbeycolor.

Market Street, left-hand side, from left to right: John Bromley's ironmongery, R.V. Bromley's footwear, Whittingham's grocery shop (with the sun blind), Roberts' leather and sports shop run by A.D. Drake, the Gas Service Centre, Slaney's Vaults, Norman Jellyman's men's outfitters, S.A.L. Electrical, Salop Cleaners, Brittain's and Florence Dixon's. On the right-hand side: Pearce's garage and the Ercall Hotel. Copyright Abbeycolor.

C. & J. Roche's provisions store at 81 New Street, with Frank Sansom's furniture shop (which had been owned by Richard Poole until the late 1920s) on the left and Aston's recently constructed showroom to the right. The ring road now cuts through these properties. Copyright Abbeycolor.

Left: Maypole Dairy Company at No. 3 New Street. Maypole staff were adept at scooping loose butter from tubs and patting it into shape before wrapping it in greaseproof paper. Right: Noah Frost's bakery and provisions shop at 88 New Street, where the best bread in the area was made. The Chad Valley Wrekin Toy Works building can just be seen in the top left-hand corner. Both photographs copyright Abbeycolor.

Ivy Dickin's florists, fruiterers and greengrocers at 86 New Street, with living accommodation on the left (next to the wall of Frost's bakery). Until around 1920 this was The Three Tuns, an inn that dated back to at least 1663. The door on the right (No. 84) was that of The Little Dustpan ironmongers in the 1930s. Copyright Abbeycolor.

Left: A contemporary advertisement for Shropshire Produce in Bell Street, where wreathes were made to order. Right: Richard Brittain's 'Food Fair' in Market Square, with its Green Shield stamp incentives. Brittain's also had a rather select café, and eventually the interior was refurbished to create a small supermarket. Photograph copyright Abbeycolor.

Upper High Street, showing a row of cottages (on the left) that has now long since been demolished. The man on the left of the picture is walking past Twinney's cobblers. The entrance to Owen's pork butchers slaughter yard is in the gap (right of centre) between the cottages, beyond which was a fish and chip shop. On the right is Roma's continental delicatessen, and the pub sign is that of the Hand and Heart public house. The temporary bus stop sign was put there because of the building work that had begun behind where the photographer was standing – bus operators were annoyed because building workers kept on moving or hiding it. Sweeping the pavement outside one's house was almost obligatory. Copyright Abbeycolor.

Left: milkman Fred Treherne at the rear of his home in Victoria Avenue, with his wife Lillian, their daughter-in-law Jessie and her son William. Right: Lillian (on the right) with her sister and next-door neighbour Gladys Jones, who delivered milk with Fred. They are standing in front of one of Fred's delivery vans.

Five

Drink

It has been said that you couldn't leave one public house in Wellington without falling (by accident) into another that happened to be next door. Although it is true that until about 1930 many people made their own beer and sold it from the front rooms of their cottages, pubs were not quite so common as has been suggested. Nevertheless, there were a lot more in 1960 than there are now.

Drinking establishments have always been an integral part of most settlements; not only were they places where people of like (or opposing) views could meet, gossip and pass the time, they were also places where visitors could stay overnight, public meetings and inquests could be held and games (like cards, darts, dominoes and a wide variety of team sports) could be played.

Provision of lunchtime snacks and evening meals is really quite a recent aspect of pub life. Pubs were generally the province of men, although barmaids were present to serve drinks. Women only tended to frequent them if escorted or if they had 'fallen' in social terms. Drunkenness was common and children were not allowed inside. Many pubs had an off-license

Source of prize-winning beer, with the slogan 'First for your thirst: Wrekin Ales', the Wrekin Brewery premises in Market Street are pictured here undergoing renovation work in May 1960. The brewery owned a considerable number of public houses in Shropshire and neighbouring counties. It closed in January 1969 when production was taken over by the Greenall Whitley brewery at Wem. Copyright Abbeycolor.

door, where alcohol and cigarettes could be purchased without actually entering the licensed part of the premises. Times change.

Several of the well-known public houses present in 1960 have since been demolished (the Glebe and the Nelson) or changed their usage (the Ercall and the Lamb) or their name (the Raven, The King's Head and the Queen's Hotel). From a historical point of view, it is a pity that long-established names are altered to meaningless and banal titles in order to impart a 'trendy' image or dispel a perceived poor reputation. Image is transient, meaningless and short-termist; reputations can be improved without resorting to name changes.

The Wrekin Brewery Company, which was owned by the Murphy family (two of whom were members of the town council) until it was taken over by the Greenall Whitley group during the 1960s, was the only beer-making company present in the town at this time; others operating during the nineteenth century and into the twentieth had either closed or been taken over. Mondays and Thursdays were brewing days, a fact that was evident to anyone with a sense of smell; the wonderful aroma of fermenting beer hung over the town like a heady and invisible cloud. The company also made fizzy pop at its O.D. Murphy & Sons premises on Holyhead Road, and used drays (by now lorries as opposed to horse-drawn wagons) to deliver both beer and pop to its customers. Empty glass pop bottles were of great benefit to children as shopkeepers would refund threepence for every one that was returned to them clean and complete with its screw-top; as a result, children were often 'paid' with these bottles when simple household chores had been done satisfactorily.

The Maltings off Alexandra Road.

Owen Downey Murphy's pop works as seen across New Church Road. The surrounding walls were topped with broken glass embedded in mortar to deter intruders. The manager's former house (on the right) was on the corner of Holyhead Road.

Another view of the pop works on Holyhead Road, with the manager's former house on the corner. Both properties were sold during the mid-1960s. The pop works supplied pop to shops, youth clubs and other organizations as well as its own tied public houses.

Last orders for the eighteenth-century Lamb Inn, 1 New Street, kept by Norman Corbett in the 1950s. The property was sold by the Wrekin Brewery for £13,200 in January 1960 to Stanton's of Hednesford. It underwent refurbishment and opened in July as a self-service food store. Copyright Abbeycolor.

The Duke of Wellington, New Street, a Wrekin Brewery public house. The gap between it and Bata's shoe shop led to the Bull's Head yard and a car park beyond. Until the 1930s the triple-gabled building on the left had been the Bull's Head Hotel and P. & M. Footwear, on the right, was Keay's printers. Copyright Abbeycolor.

The Ercall Hotel, Market Street, another Wrekin Brewery hostelry, many of which ceased trading after being acquired by the Greenall Whitley group in the late 1960s and early 1970s. The entrance to the former potato market is to the left and Pearce's Ercall Garage to the right. Copyright Abbeycolor.

Bell Street, with Norman Keay's Rose & Crown pub between Myladi's and Blakeley's shoe and clothing shop. The Barley Mow is before the gap (leading to Espley's slaughter yard) at the far end of the street on the left. Pointon's decorating premises lie beyond Shropshire Produce on the right. Copyright Abbeycolor.

The Fox & Hounds, an Ind Coope & Allsopp brewery-tied house in Crown Street. The parking sign directs motorists to the Belmont Hall car park, which could be accessed through a narrow opening immediately after Chetwood's Garage in Tan Bank. Copyright Abbeycolor.

Left: High Street. From left to right: Ernest Corbett & Son's shoe retail and repair shop, their house next door and the Duke's Head (known as 'The Bottles'). Right: Slaney's Vaults – one of the oldest alcohol businesses in the town at the time – in Market Square. Both photographs copyright Abbeycolor.

The Queen's Hotel on the corner of Walker Street, one of several public houses to subsequently be renamed in an attempt to reinvent itself and attract a different type of customer. Copyright Abbeycolor.

S.K. Williams Ltd's wine shop and off licence on the corner of Church Street and Plough Road. Doctors Bambridge, Pooler and Hewatt-Jaboor's surgery was in The Villa, which was on the other side of Church Street opposite the cottages on the left. Copyright Abbeycolor.

Left: J. Whittingham's grocery store in Market Street. Right: E.M. Brocklesby's 'corner' shop in High Street; property to the left had already been demolished and time was ticking away. The site of Brocklesby's is now occupied by part of Keay Flats. Both photographs copyright Abbeycolor.

W.J. Laud's confectionery shop in Market Approach. Laud's actual bakery was in Wrekin Road. The iron gates on the left of the picture were closed and locked on non-market days to ensure that the market hall was secure. Copyright Abbeycolor.

Six

Reading and Refreshment

Two aspects of life in 1960 Wellington go hand-in-hand. People enjoyed reading anything and everything, including books, newspapers, comics (which child can ever forget the *Dandy, Beano, Topper, Beezer, Eagle, Lion, Tiger, Wizard* and, especially for girls, *Bunty, Princess, School Friend* and *Girls Crystal?*) and American publications like *Classics Illustrated, Superman* etc.

Daily newspapers were of course the most popular, and were the only means by which fish and chips should be wrapped. The evening paper at the time was the Wolverhampton-based *Express and Star*, the local office of which was in Tan Bank. Saturdays were noted for the weekly *Sporting Pink*. Thursdays were awaited with some anticipation because that was when the incomparable *Wellington Journal & Shrewsbury News*, full of local reports, hit the streets. One of

Nona Woollam's newsagents at 10 Crown Street, where all manner of publications, cigarettes and sweets were on sale. Bessie Ruston (left) worked here, occasionally assisted by Margaret Gregory, whose main job was in Nona's haberdashery shop in Duke Street; the joint premises ran through from one street to the other.

the 'free' (with a nominal price of one penny) papers delivered to every home in the town was the *Quality Advertiser*, an economy, no-frills publication produced by D. Vaughan and G. Bebb, wherein businesses could advertise their services and members of the public place 'For Sale' and 'Wanted' ads. Magazines were also read with enthusiasm. Light-content regulars like *People's Friend* (with its knitting patterns), *Woman*, *Woman's Own*, *Punch* etc. would appear on tables in doctors' waiting rooms soon after publication, whereas 'worthwhile' offerings like *Do It Yourself*, *Practical Householder* (this was the Age of Formica) and *Amateur Photographer* were retained by enthusiasts as sources of reference. Comic-like booklets featuring westerns and wartime escapades were popular reading among men. The main and children's public libraries in Walker Street were frequented by many and paperbacks could be bought relatively cheaply at W.H. Smith's and other newsagents.

Folk also enjoyed a good chat over a cup (not mug!) of coffee and a fancy cake in the morning, or tea if they happened to be in town in the afternoon. Both reading and refreshment were well catered for in Wellington, except on Sundays – then the centre of the town was as dead as the grave and almost devoid of life apart from churchgoers, newspaper buyers or roaming dogs. It was practically impossible to buy anything apart from petrol – and even that

QUALITY ADVERTISER

UNION ROAD, WELLINGTON.　　　TEL. 1134

Xmas Gift Problem Solved

Get the Unforgetable Gift from:

C. ALLBUTT & Co. Ltd

9, MILL BANK, WELLINGTON. PHONE: 797

Useful and Fancy Electrical Goods that will give Pleasure throughout the year

Issue 17, 1st. Year	DECEMBER 3rd 1960.	Price One Penny

Quality Advertiser *masthead. This was a useful publication. Besides having trade and private advertisements it also carried information on social events and poems by Wellingtonian Norman Williams.*

The Wellington Journal & Shrewsbury News *offices in Church Street. Copyright Abbeycolor.*

wasn't guaranteed – or ice cream from one of the then new-fangled vans with the irritating chimes. Traders in the town were obliged to adhere to the Sunday trading laws, so purchases were limited mainly to newspapers and whatever else newsagents sold (until they closed at lunchtime), and emergency medicines from the 'duty pharmacy' (chemists operated a rota system).

A new café on The Parade car park following the demolition of the Robin Hood British Restaurant (which had occupied the site of the present public conveniences from 1943 until the late 1950s) was requested but, as Sunday bus and train services were few and very far between, it wasn't considered worth the expense. It was a similar story on Wednesdays after one o'clock, when half-day closing brought the town to an almost complete standstill. As a general rule, opening times for most shops on other days were from 9 a.m. until 5 p.m. Even banks and the Tax Office observed these times, although they closed at lunchtime on Saturdays.

Nevertheless, the town had more than enough cafés of varying standard to meet the needs of its customers. Pubs tended not to serve coffee but no woman in her right mind would pass through their doors unescorted anyway. Cafés were excellent places to meet and gossip. People had their own preferences: Jay's in Queen Street was used mainly by passengers awaiting Midland Red buses; Heath's attracted slightly better off customers; The Square and Sidoli's cafés were clean and friendly; Brittain's seemed more like an old English tea room; Jervis's catered for Association bus drivers and conductresses as well as passing shoppers (it was a long walk to the Dawley Road council estate). The YMCA building and billiards hall in Tan Bank had snack bars – even the Market Hall had a café which operated from a caravan inside the Market Approach entrance. Most churches also had Saturday coffee mornings for members of their congregations.

Coffee, tea and fancy cakes were an essential part of Wellington life.

W.H. Smith's stationery store in Market Square with the Midland Bank to the left before the Station Road turning. Smith's was the only real bookseller in Wellington in 1960. Hobson's, diagonally opposite in the Square, was finding it increasingly difficult to compete with Smith's greater range and keenly-priced stationery. Strangely enough though, Hobson's shop managed to outlive Smith's, although the latter's presence in the town has since returned and now has premises at the railway bridge corner of Market Square. Copyright Abbeycolor.

Miss Frances Baxter's newsagents at Medical Hall, Church Street, which was formerly one of Tom Austin's shops in the town. Miss Baxter was also a grocer and chemist. Copyright Abbeycolor.

Left: Heath's confectionery and catering shop in New Street, inside which lay an upmarket restaurant and café, later named the 'Rainbow Room'. Next door was Mary Heath's haberdashery and knitwear shop. Right: Jervis's café in High Street, frequented by bus drivers and shoppers alike. Next door was Austin's newsagents owned by Hubert and Alice Case; Hubert ('Bert') was a town councillor. Both photographs copyright Abbeycolor.

Cliff Jervis with his ice cream van in the late 1950s. Jervis's home-made ice cream was second to none (although some preferred Sidoli's). Cliff also drove his father's buses.

Cliff's sister, Daisy Jervis, serving snacks and hot and cold drinks from behind the counter of the High Street café. Daisy's father John transferred his bus company from Wrockwardine Wood to Wellington around 1930. He and Daisy formed an accordian duo during the 1930s and played at concerts and variety shows throughout the area.

Left: The Square Café in Market Square, where boxes of chocolates and fancy cakes could also be bought. Right: Jack Ward's newsagents in New Street (next to Aston's new furniture showroom) with Jack Nicholls' small butchers shop to the right. Both photographs copyright Abbeycolor.

Fancy cakes, ice cream and chocolate: all could be obtained from Sidoli's café in New Street between Onion's butchers and K.J. wallpapers and paints. Sidoli's, owned by the Bassini family, prided itself on cleanliness and good waitress service. It was a popular meeting place for shoppers and amorous couples. Copyright Abbeycolor.

Left: Avery Scales and Case's (formerly Hesketh's) Fish & Chip 'restaurant', Nos 1 and 3 High Street. Right: rejected by the people: Kipp's Café at 80 New Street, awaiting demolition. The café – which was little more than a gay bar – had closed in the early 1950s because it attracted 'the wrong type of customers'. 1960 Wellington wasn't ready for that sort of thing. Both photographs copyright Abbeycolor.

THE FOREST GLEN PAVILION

THE WREKIN
near WELLINGTON

We cater for all BANQUETS, WEDDINGS and ORGANISED PARTIES. Seating for up to 200 guests.

●

One of Shropshire's famous beauty spots — an ideal centre for your Spring and Summer Outings.

●

Established 1889 by the same family as the present Proprietors,

MR. & MRS. P. E. POINTON

●

Telephone Wellington 363

The Forest Glen Pavilion in a 1960 advertisement. The Pavilion was a popular venue for formal evening dinner dances and daytime refreshments for Wrekin Hill walkers and sightseers. The building was filled with deer's heads, china and cabinets full of stuffed birds and animals such as foxes and stoats. At least the food was fresh!

51

Norman Jellyman's gents' and boys' outfitters at 4 New Street. Norman was forced to abandon these premises at the beginning of 1960 because they were to be demolished to widen the road and make space for new premises for C.D. Jones, ladies' and children's clothing. Before this, Mrs Jones' small shop was in Crown Street. Craddocks, a long-established footwear store, is on the extreme right. Boots the chemist was at 2 New Street.

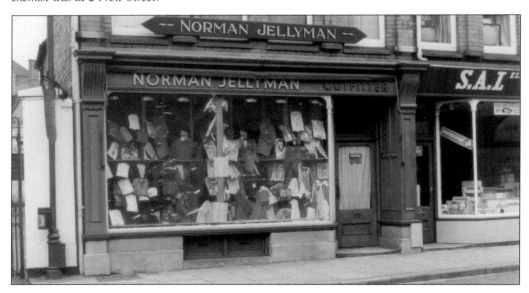

By May 1960, Norman Jellyman had moved to these premises in Market Street. The gated entrance to Slaney's Vaults trade counter (their licensed premises were in Market Square) is to the left. S.A.L. Electrical is to the right. Copyright Abbeycolor.

Seven

Fashion

Wellington was not without its fashion shops, catering for every pocket (there were always church rummage sales for those with limited means). Although market stalls stocked cheap-and-cheerful ranges of clothing, many people tended to favour the town's outfitters who provided better quality attire.

The clothing market was well defined. Some shops catered for men and boys, others for ladies, girls and babies. Schoolchildren in most of Wellington's schools were required to wear a uniform and school sports kit from about age seven onwards. Uniforms not only let people know who was misbehaving in public but also provided some equality among pupils themselves; they all looked the same, however well off or poor their parents were. Uniforms kept vanity and one-upmanship in check; furthermore, they helped to encourage a feeling of pride in belonging to a particular school.

Jellyman's (in Market Street), Bradley's (Market Square) and Agnew's and Steventon's (Church Street), were among the shops supplying uniforms for boys and school ties for both girls and boys. Gaberdine macintoshes (with detachable underjackets) were the norm for most

Agnew's outfitters shop in Church Street. The passage on the left, between it and the recently-moved Valeting Service, led to the printing works of the Wellington Journal & Shrewsbury News *and Margaret Kendrick's School of Dance. The* Journal *offices were to the right of Agnew's. Copyright Abbeycolor.*

Market Square. From left to right: Hepworths, Pearks's provisions, Hiltons shoes and J.C. Lloyd's high class provisions. Copyright Abbeycolor.

Lower New Street. From left to right: Johnsons' cleaners, Baxters' butchers, Craddocks' shoes and F.R. Burton's chemists (where photographic equipment was also sold) followed by F.W. Woolworth & Co. Ltd. C.D. Jones' new shop was being built behind the temporary hoarding on the right. Copyright Abbeycolor.

children, whatever the weather, although duffle coats (with wooden toggles that had a tendency to drop off) were gaining popularity. Outfitters also acted as agents for the essential Cash's woven name labels that mothers had to sew into every item (including caps, berets, socks and underwear) that their offspring might take to school.

Young men wishing to acquire that man-about-town look favoured Hepworths for their suits and Blakeley's or Bradley's for jeans and other casual wear. Winkle-pickers were (sensibly) on the way out; the teddy boy look had all but disappeared by 1960 (although Brylcreem-sleeked hair was still highly popular), so feet had a chance to resume their normal shape. Hush Puppy suede shoes were on the way in, as were Tuf rubber-soled shoes for boys; the hob nailed boot was almost extinct in the school playground, a sure sign that living standards were improving.

Women's magazines, as ever, encouraged the fairer sex, whatever their age, to succumb to the vagaries and temptations of fashion. (Such things were beyond most men. Clothes are clothes.) And it wasn't just outer garments. Myladi's and Lana's were foremost in displaying weird and flimsy ranges of the latest underwear in their shop windows. Most youths could only dream of their purpose but, once they understood the role of suspenders, relied heavily on having a ready supply of 'tanner' coins (sixpenny pieces) in case a wayward stocking began to slip teasingly down its owner's leg on the dance floor when a fitting sprang off the elastic. Tights, those highly functional enemies of the red-blooded male (or so he thought), had yet to appear; nylon stockings that laddered for no apparent reason were still in.

There were a few higher-class outfitters capable of measuring clients and tailoring bespoke garments; Ann Windsor at 10 Mill Bank and Shrewsbury-based Alberta Batsford's in Walker Street catered for ladies who wanted something exclusive. Hepworths and Steventon's also provided a similar service in men's suits, as did other outfitters at this time, although most sales were 'off the peg'.

C.D. Jones' ladies' and children's clothing shop at No. 1 Crown Street. The reflection of George Mason's provisions shop over the road can be seen in the window. Copyright Abbeycolor.

A.E. Beard's butchers and one of Florence Dixon's ladies' fashion shops in New Street. Florence Dixon also had premises in Market Street between Brittain's and G.W. Harvey's jewellery store. The poster on the door advertises a fashion show to be held on 25 May 1960, organized by the staff of Wellington Telephone Exchange. Copyright Abbeycolor.

Lana's 'separates' ladies' clothing store in Market Square, with the premises of the former Lamb Inn undergoing refurbishment to the right at No. 1 New Street. Copyright Abbeycolor.

Myladi's store on the corner of New and Bell Streets. Like Lana's, this was one of those places where ladies shopped and the male population could only imagine. Copyright Abbeycolor.

Located between the YMCA building and the Raven Hotel in Walker Street, the upmarket Alberta Batsford Ltd sold tasteful branded garments to discerning customers. A Dereta 'Paris curl', pure wool, voluminous, striking top coat with an opulent Persian lamb collar cost as much as nineteen guineas. Copyright Abbeycolor.

Buy clothing and hats or buy material to make your own. For the latter, Dafferns, like McClures, sold everything you might need at their shop next door to Heath's in New Street. Copyright Abbeycolor.

Knitting and embroidery were very well catered for in the town. Mary Teresa Gray's shop in Market Street (left) and Nona Woollam's store in Duke Street (right) provided a wide range of knitting, needlework and haberdashery products. Nona also sold dress 'accompaniments' like handbags. Both photographs copyright Abbeycolor.

McClures' ladies' department in Duke Street. The company, which began in 1908, also had a soft furnishings and drapery department over the road, which ran through to Crown Street. Cash payment for goods was put into a wooden container attached to an overhead cable, which shot it into the cash office at the rear of the shop. Change would come back via the same route. To the left is Chatfield's grocery shop, formerly owned by Mr Fifield. Copyright Abbeycolor.

McClures' men's department (the ladies' department was to the left of the alley) in Duke Street. Unless they were closing down, shops only had two sales a year: one in January ('winter') and the other in July ('summer'). In front of the shop are, from left to right: Elsie Evans (ladies' fashion), Margaret Jones (cashier) and Daphne Roberts (ladies' accessories).

Left: Bean's shop (opposite Dewhurst's butchers) in New Street. Right: Steventon's (with see-through blinds) in Church Street. Both photographs copyright Abbeycolor.

Gardeners were particularly well catered for at Briscoe's ironmongers (61 High Street, left) and Pritchard's seed stores (Market Hall, right). Both photographs copyright Abbeycolor.

Eight

Doing It Yourself

The 1950s had seen the arrival of more readily available, affordable and versatile tools intended for the Do It Yourself market. Furthermore, Wellington Urban District Council had, during the same period, encouraged housing development, not only in large council estates but also in properties intended specifically for private buyers. These facts, combined with captivating illustrations in *Do It Yourself* and *Practical Woodworking* magazines, supported the view that home improvements were possible in every home. Post-war standards of living had already risen considerably; more people than hitherto had decent accommodation in which to live; the next step was to maintain those properties and, somehow, personalize them. It made little difference to the occupants whether homes were privately or council owned when it came to improving their surroundings.

Wellington had catered well for skilled tradesmen even before the railway came to the town in 1849. Everything needed to build, alter or improve property was on hand. The single most noticeable factor by 1960 was that there was an increasing tendency for doing it yourself rather

The Red House, High Street, occupied by W. Johnson & Sons' ironmongers. A delivery van was kept in the garage on the left with the arched door, and the family's living area was accessed through the door on the right-hand side of the building. Christ Church tower can be seen behind property which was, until around 1930, the Red Lion pub. Copyright Abbeycolor.

than employing the sometimes expensive (although considerably more adept) services of one of the town's tradesmen. Some of those tradesmen (for example, painter and decorator Ronald Purcell in Tan Bank) not only could do the work but also opened shops from which customers wishing to try their hand at doing things for themselves could purchase all the essentials. Decorating in many older houses meant pasting another layer over the existing wallpaper because the plaster beneath was prone to disintegrate, and re-varnishing heavily embossed paper up the stairway wall.

Other shops, like K.J. Wallpapers and Rose & Co. in New Street, catered specifically for domestic clients and displayed rolls of wall coverings and paint charts to help the decision-making process. More to the point, customers could make immediate purchases. Older establishments, catering more for the professional market, tended to keep wallpaper sample books and placed orders with the manufacturers; while deliveries might be relatively speedy, it was inevitably slower than buying goods off the shelf.

Decorating was one thing: more ambitious projects were often beyond the capabilities of most people, especially those involving regulatory legislation. Nevertheless, many were tempted to save money by avoiding the perceived high cost of employing a professional and were well catered for by specialist businesses, including York's (in New Street) and Pearce's (in Market Street), both of which had many years of experience in their particular fields. Times change and, by 1960, their customers included a growing number of ordinary people in addition to traditional tradesfolk.

Most of the staff serving in these DIY shops were able to give sound advice; shop assistants took pride in their jobs and actually knew a great deal about the products they sold, often gained through their own practical experience. Of course, not every domestic project was successful and sometimes had to be abandoned through lack of ability and knowledge. In those circumstances, there was little choice but to employ the services of a professional to rectify matters.

And Jim Rollason, at his scrap yard premises in High Street, was always on hand to give some recompense for all the wasted and mangled brass, copper and lead amassed by professionals and amateurs alike.

Arthur Pearce & Sons' building supplies company in Market Street, which sold everything from cement and sand for building foundations to timber and tiles for roofing, including everything (baths, sinks, etc.) in between. Copyright Abbeycolor.

Friendly and always helpful to DIYers: Harry Edwards in the entrance to the machine shop at the rear of Harry Edwards & Sons' premises in High Street. Their Do It Yourself Stores opened in the mid-1960s. Harry and his brothers Tom and Frank were also the most respected funeral undertakers in the town.

This John Bromley electrical engineering store in Market Street had just closed when this photograph was taken, the business having recently moved to much larger premises in Bridge Road to concentrate on agricultural engineering. The company had also previously rented a small shop in Walker Street but this had already been vacated by this time. The words painted on the wall refer to G. Pierce's former Cycle Works, in business from about 1900. Copyright Abbeycolor.

Pointon's plumbing and decorating supplies shop in Crown Street. The premises extended through to Bell Street behind. To the left is Gwynne's, a small hairdressing and drapery shop at 5 Crown Street. Copyright Abbeycolor.

Walter Davies & Son on the corner of Walker and Duke Streets. The store stocked an incredible range of Wolf and other well-known brands' power tools and hardware (nails and screws were sold loose by weight) as well as glass, Formica and some timber. They served both trade and domestic customers. Copyright Abbeycolor.

G.H. York & Co., one of the largest plumbing and heating engineering businesses in the town with two double-fronted shops in New Street flanking the entrance to a service yard at the rear. York's not only supplied everything needed by domestic and trade customers (such as specialist tools, pipes, radiators, boilers, baths, sinks, tiles, paint and wallpaper) but they also sold a wide range of appliances for kitchens and bathrooms. Both photographs copyright Abbeycolor.

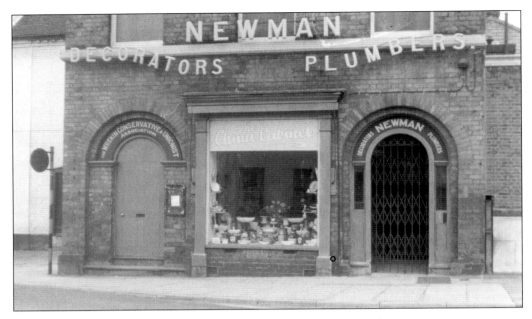

Newman's decorating and plumbing business at 8 Church Street. Mr Newman's wife ran the China Cabinet on the premises, selling glass and porcelain giftware. The Wrekin Conservative and Unionist Association office was next door; their agent was E.J. Dockerill. Cawthorne's jewellery shop was in the white building set back on the left. Copyright Abbeycolor.

K.J. wallpapers and paints in New Street, between Sidoli's café to the left and Bates & Hunts chemists to the right. Copyright Abbeycolor.

Professional decorator Ronald Purcell ran this Tan Bank store, which had a workshop at the rear. He was assisted by his son Bryan, who later took over the business. The Purcells also had a small sweet shop here between 1929 and 1958. Copyright Abbeycolor.

Left: the New Street branch of Rose's decorating; Curry's was to the right. Right: if domestic attempts at plumbing and rewiring failed dismally, Jim Rollason's scrap yard in High Street was the place to recover some of the high cost of metal, especially brass, lead and copper. Both photographs copyright Abbeycolor.

The Midlands Electricity Board showroom on the corner of Walker Street and Tan Bank, where customers could examine a wide range of clean, efficient and labour-saving domestic appliances. Work was well under way on a new building (which can be seen on the left) in Tan Bank, intended for use by the Express and Star evening newspaper. The entrance to the YMCA building is to the right. Copyright Abbeycolor.

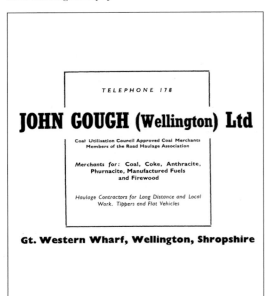

TELEPHONE 178

JOHN GOUGH (Wellington) Ltd

Coal Utilisation Council Approved Coal Merchants
Members of the Road Haulage Association

Merchants for: Coal, Coke, Anthracite,
Phurnacite, Manufactured Fuels
and Firewood

Haulage Contractors for Long Distance and Local
Work. Tippers and Flat Vehicles

Gt. Western Wharf, Wellington, Shropshire

Left: a contemporary advertisement for one of the town's many coal merchants, some of whom occupied premises conveniently situated next to the railway sidings. Right: the National Coal Board showroom and office in Tan Bank. Purcell's decorating store was to the left. Photograph copyright Abbeycolor.

Nine

Fuel and Finance

By 1960 Wellington had been supplied with gas for well over a century (the first gas works company was established in March 1851, although gas had been produced privately for several years beforehand); until the 1940s when electricity took over, it had been the dominant means by which the streets and people's homes were illuminated. The gas works in 1960, with three enormous containers built by C. & W. Walker of Donnington, were located near Alexandra and Hollies Roads. The premises were a popular venue for group visits from various organizations in Wellington and the surrounding area, who attended not only to witness how coal produced, for example, gas and coke, but also to learn about the many products (including nylon stockings) that were made using the by-products generated by certain chemical processes.

In spite of press advertisements promoting gas fires, coal was still the traditional source of heat, although gas cookers had long since replaced black ranges in most kitchens. Coal was cheap, and was delivered in open-backed lorries straight to the coal shed by black-faced coalmen, who oddly enough did not wear the expected neckerchief around their necks, although some did wear cloth caps and sleeveless leather jackets.

The Gas Service Centre, which was next to Roberts' leather goods and sports shop in Market Street. Mr Woodfine was the manager at the Centre for many years. Copyright Abbeycolor.

Electricity, which was cheap and reliable, was by then the main source of lighting. Electric cookers and fires were available but were more expensive to run than gas. Advertising claims that electricity was cleaner (which it was) could not counter the fact that it was also more expensive. Eventually, the proverbial Joneses would adopt electric cookers and fires, thus ensuring that at least some of their neighbours would follow suit, but the Midlands Electricity Board showroom was for the time being fighting an uphill battle. As with the gas works, organized trips to the Central Generating Board power station on the river Severn at Buildwas were arranged for the populace to be amazed at such wonderful technology. The trouble with electricity was that it could not be seen or heard, and not many people understood how it worked, whereas folk knew where they were with coal and gas.

Visits to the Granville and Grange coal mines at Donnington Wood were, understandably, few and far between owing to safety implications. Then, as now (except that coal is difficult to find and just as difficult to use because of the proliferation of smokeless zones), the choice between electricity, coal or gas for specific purposes in the home rested with the consumer.

Money matters have always been of great interest to people, especially those who have little of it. 'Professionals' are always ready to give advice on where and how money should be invested or borrowed. One major difference between 1960 and the present is that back then credit was at best difficult and at worst impossible to get; credit cards had yet to be invented. Hire purchase was the normal way to acquire larger, more expensive household furniture and appliances; very few people could afford to pay the full amount in cash or by cheque. Overdrafts were difficult to obtain and expensive to repay, even though interest rates were relatively low. A mortgage was the only debt some people had. If they couldn't afford something, they went without or saved up over a period of time. Impulse buying was a rare phenomenon.

Thompson's, opposite Woolworths in New Street, was at this time still acting as a pawnbroker,

Gas board staff enjoying their annual dinner dance in December 1960. Muriel Bishop and Jean Windsor sit sixth and seventh from the left on the front table. Muriel was a very talented artist and from the early 1940s onwards had devoted most of her spare time to nursing activities in the district, for which she received many awards.

although with wages gradually rising, the number of regular visitors was tailing off dramatically. For once it was possible to save a little 'for a rainy day'. This trend had become more noticeable after the end of the Second World War, when women were understandably reluctant to give up their jobs and their new-found freedom. Families were able to live a little less frugally than they had done before. They might even have enough to take the family away to a holiday camp, rather than sitting at home or visiting relatives in Southport or Wolverhampton. Or they might be able to buy (or more likely rent, because of their unreliability) a television.

The Second World War had encouraged people to save as part of the war effort. When the war ended, banks saw the opportunity to promote continued regular saving and devised various schemes to encourage customers. As a result, new or refurbished branch offices appeared; one of which was the Trustee Savings Bank in Walker Street, renovated in 1956. The types of accounts available were quite limited compared with today's, and a lot less confusing. Although obviously in business to make a profit, banks were content to provide a good service without attempting to hide charges or deceive their customers; they maintained an air of honesty and respectability.

The TSB introduced a Savings Stamp scheme at schools in the town, whereby teachers collected small amounts of cash from pupils and gave them stamps featuring Prince Charles and Princess Anne to stick in a small booklet until enough had been collected to take to the bank for payment into a deposit account. All transactions were carried out painstakingly by hand; computations were limited to the facilities of hand-cranked adding machines.

Banks were useful for saving amounts that were to be readily accessible. Insurance Societies promoted long-term investments, and of course life assurance; the Second World War was sufficiently fresh in most folks' minds for them to understand the suffering, misery and hardship resulting from an unexpected bereavement. So, like the banks and building societies, insurance companies opened new offices and employed agents (often local accountants and solicitors) to raise their profile. Most business was conducted in customers' homes by agents collecting and entering small premiums in a payment book. Insurance companies also benefitted from the legal requirement for motorists to insure their vehicles.

The pawnbrokers on New Street. The business had been owned by H. Wilkes until George Thompson (Carnforth) Ltd acquired it in 1903. Pawning and redeeming valuables was going out of fashion so the company was obliged to concentrate more on selling affordable household furnishings and domestic ware. Copyright Abbeycolor.

The Trustee Savings Bank branch office in Walker Street. R.C. Rawlings's accountant's office is through the door on the extreme left. Rawlings also acted as agent for Leeds Permanent Building Society. The house on the right was a private dwelling, but is now an opticians. Copyright Abbeycolor.

The Midland Bank at the corner of Station Road (to the left) and Market Square. Copyright Abbeycolor.

Walker Street. On the left-hand side is the flat-roofed Prudential Assurance office, then Gwynne's solicitors, beyond which are gates leading into the Wrekin Brewery loading yard. On the right is Roper's builders yard on the corner of Wrekin Road, followed by a long row of condemned properties leading to the public library before the bend in the road. Copyright Abbeycolor.

Church Street, with Lloyds Bank to the left of Valeting Services. The Journal *offices occupy the corner with Queen Street to the right and All Saints parish churchyard is in the left foreground. Copyright Abbeycolor.*

Left: Wesleyan and General Assurance Society office at No. 4 High Street. Right: one of several small electrical appliance service and repair shops, this one in Walker Street. Both photographs copyright Abbeycolor.

COUNTRY COOKING
COMES TO TOWN

hot baths
galore, too—
with a
RAYBURN
solid fuel
cooker!

RAYBURN COOKERS BY ALLIED IRONFOUNDERS

THE SHROPSHIRE FIREPLACE CO.
35/37 High Street
WELLINGTON
Tel. 1222

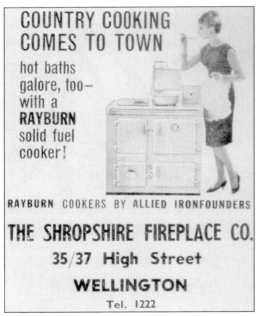

Left: a late 1960 advertisement for a newly-built shop that had opened in June in High Street. Independent stores were an alternative to buying domestic appliances from the fuel-supply board shops. Right: Collis Radio at 2 Market Street, next to George Harvey's jewellery shop. Photograph copyright Abbeycolor.

Ten

Clean and Tidy

Four things in particular stand out as being essential to improving and maintaining one's public appearance: clean clothes, tidy hair, good health and spectacles (if you need them). The Wellington of 1960 catered for every one of these.

Two arguments have been put forward to account for the relatively high number of cleaners in the town. The first is that not every household possessed a washing machine (although stores like E.W. Jones were doing their best to change the situation); the second is that newer fashions and bedding fabrics should not undergo the normal wet washing experience in case they shrank or fell apart in the wash. Consequently, three types of cleaning service were available: steam, wet and dry.

Of course, most washing was done domestically (and usually on Mondays); if a home did not have a washing machine (sometimes fitted with a labour-saving mangle), cleaning had to be done using tubs and dollies, which was highly labour-intensive. Furthermore, washing had to be hung outside or, if the weather was inclement, from a pulley-operated rack suspended from the kitchen ceiling; tumble-dryers were still a thing of the future.

Some articles do not lend themselves to washing at home, which is why specialist shops were frequented. Suits, overcoats, dresses, curtains and even ties were taken to the cleaner's. Dry

Market Square looking towards Duke Street. E.W. Jones not only supplied large and small electrical appliances but also hi-fi record players, reel-to-reel tape recorders, transcription units, records, televisions and radios (transistors were becoming more reliable). Market Approach is beyond Wrekin Cleaners, which opened in March. Bradley's outfitters is on the left, next to the rear entrance of Boots the chemist by the van. Copyright Abbeycolor.

Left: Dry-cleaning methods were employed by Quality Cleaners in New Street. Right: traditional washing was done by F.W. Chen at Mann's Chinese Laundry at 47 High Street. Both photographs copyright Abbeycolor.

Wellington Cleaners in Market Square. The door on the right leads up to Central Chambers where solicitor R.A. Clarke had his office. The painted iron support pole at Stead & Simpson's shoe shop, on the left, was put there to prevent damage being done by vehicles negotiating the tight corner into Market Street. Copyright Abbeycolor.

cleaning was still in its infancy; at the same time, traditional laundries were either having to change their cleaning techniques or face the prospect of the business failing. Dry cleaning was much faster; items could be ready for collection the next day, if not sooner. Wet or, more accurately, steam laundries usually had a three-day turnaround; many customers still preferred some articles, especially bed sheets, to be hand washed, and were prepared to wait. Self-service laundrettes had yet to be realized.

The oldest, longest-seving steam laundry was undoubtedly Wellington Cleaners, whose main 'receiving' depot was in Prince's Street (the part sometimes referred to as 'school lane'). The business began in 1893 under the joint ownership of William and Martha Bentley. By the mid-1950s, a van collected and delivered washing not only from its shops in Market Street, Wellington, and Haybridge Road, Hadley, but also visited its regular customers' homes. The Wellington branch of Mann's Chinese Laundry was just one of thousands spread across Britain at this time, but it would not be many more years before the chain died out.

A visit to the hairdresser (or barber in the case of men – 'hairdressing' was for women only) was an important social event for women. It could mean hours under a domed dryer reading magazines and gossiping between cigarettes and cups of tea. Saturday was the most popular day to pay a visit, and with the hair freshly permed, lacquered or wrapped in a headscarf (possibly still with plastic rollers in place) was often followed by shopping before returning home to have their (weekly) bath in readiness for a night out. Hairdressers often had windows adorned with frilly lace curtains.

Men, on the other hand, tended to see a haircut as a much-begrudged necessity prompted by comments from a wife or mother. Again, Saturdays were extremely busy for barbers, especially during the hours leading up to a football match at the Buck's Head ground or a lunchtime drink in the local. Or both.

Left: Salop Cleaners at 6 High Street (which was next to the Wesleyan and General Assurance Society). Right: Qualitie Klene in one of the Market Hall retail outlets in Market Street, opposite the Gas Service Centre. 'Clever' (i.e. bad) spelling of the trade name was a portent of things to come. Both photographs copyright Abbeycolor.

Richards' hairdressing shop in Market Square between Brittain's two stores. Richards also sold tobacco products as did most, if not all, of the other hairdressers in the town. Notice the early vending machine. Copyright Abbeycolor.

Left: Cecil Clifford's barbers and umbrella repair shop, High Street. Old cottages on the left had just been demolished to build new premises for Avery Scales and Shropshire Fireplaces. Right: John Henry Jones had been a bootmaker at this shop from the 1880s until the 1940s. By 1960 it was Janette's hairdressers, run by Mrs Pickering. The archway to the left leads to the Nelson Inn yard and some small cottages. Both photographs copyright Abbeycolor.

Chemist's shops were required to supply products serving the illnesses (and vanities, and hobbies) of Wellington's expanding population. Despite the specialist nature of the business, all were obliged to sell non-pharmaceutical products in order to survive economically. Boots was a branch of a national concern and was able to benefit from bulk ordering of supplies. Frances Baxter's at Medical Hall was, like the rest, very much a local concern, and sold newspapers and groceries as well as medicines. Burton's specialized in camera equipment and dark room supplies. Bates & Hunt had two shops, one of which stocked an excellent range of wine- and beer-making products; the Bates and Hunt partnership was formed in around 1903, at which time James Bates was also a grocer. Picture Book, chemists, have been associated with photography ever since the hobby became less mysterious towards the end of the nineteenth century; it relied, after all, on chemistry for its success.

Eye tests, which until the 1940s had often been administered by jewellers, were now being conducted by opticians, like Mr Thorley who worked at Luckings in Crown Street (where the optician's had previously been the jeweller's G.W. Harvey), Lawrence Shinn in Market Square and D.D. Mawson in Tan Bank.

A 1960 advertisement for Mawson, the Tan Bank optician.

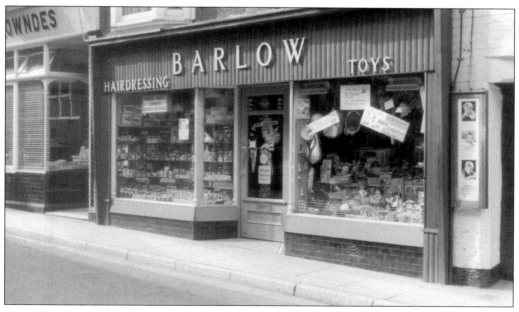

Barlow's in New Street not only styled hair but also sold a wonderful range of toys including Bayco building sets and Hornby Dublo trains and accessories. The door on the extreme right leads upstairs to Wrekin Photo Services, which had studios above both Barlow's and Lowndes' butchers shop on the left. Copyright Abbeycolor.

Left: Jose Grant's hairdressing shop, which was once The Queen's Head public house, next to Jack Nicholls' butchers shop in New Street. Right: Mayfair Salon in New Street; Allum's owned this, and a jewellery shop to its left. Both photographs copyright Abbeycolor.

Whiteways hairdressers in Church Street. The first houses in Park Street are to the left. Vineyard Road, now extended to join King Street, runs through where these properties stood. Copyright Abbeycolor.

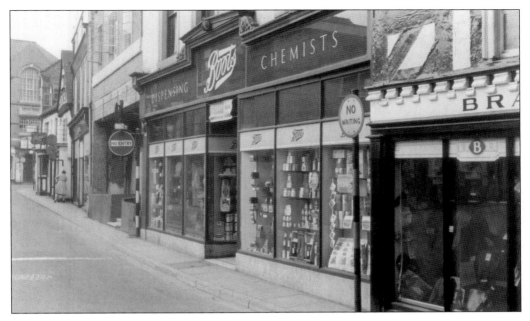

Boots at No. 2 New Street, sandwiched between George Mason's grocers (undergoing refurbishment) at the entrance to Crown Street and Bradley's outfitters in Market Square. The woman on the left is standing between McClures drapery and soft furnishings shop and the White Lion public house. Copyright Abbeycolor.

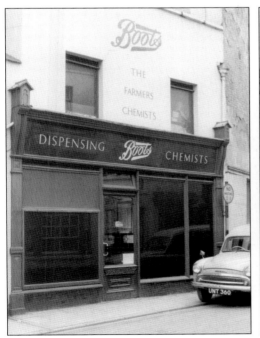

Left: Boots' rear entrance on Duke Street. Right: Bates & Hunt's Market Square chemists shop. Both photographs copyright Abbeycolor.

Bates & Hunt's chemists shop in New Street. As well as the usual array of pharmaceutical and healthcare products, wine and beer making equipment and photographic supplies were also sold here. Films (black and white only) 'for faces and places' could be bought out of hours from the vending machine. Copyright Abbeycolor.

Luckings' opticians in Crown Street between the site of the Crown public house, now incorporated into the offices of Wellington News, and Gwynne's former hairdressing and drapery shop. Copyright Abbeycolor.

Eleven
More No More

It will be evident from earlier pages that the face of Wellington has altered substantially over the last forty years. This chapter is something of a 'mopping up' exercise. Again, it shows properties that have been converted for different uses, businesses that have succumbed to economic change or the retirements of owners' and roads that have been dramatically altered or no longer exist.

Not all the changes have been good; Wellington in 1960 had more than a hint of character, but years of neglect and poorly-conceived 'trendy' planning decisions have resulted in the loss of several notable social and economic landmarks.

Norah Wellings' Victoria Toy Works in King Street went on sale in 1960. It had closed the year before following the death of Norah's brother in 1958; he had been her mentor and manager since the factory began in the mid-1920s, and she found it impossible to continue without him. Norah had previously been employed as a designer for the Chad Valley Company in New Street. (For more information see The Chad Valley Wrekin Toy Works and Noah Frost's Bakery Row *by the same author.) While the Chad Valley catered for the mass market, Norah's quality dolls were made specifically for people who could afford expensive luxuries, notably cruise-liner passengers and Harrod's customers in London. In 1931, the Chad Valley, seeing Norah's success, made overtures to merge the two businesses; they were politely rejected. To the left is the Baptist chapel: production began here but eventually expanded into the purpose-built central area. The offices were on the right. Even a caretaker's house (Fairfield Cottage) was provided.*

Luxitours office, on the left, was a forerunner in promoting vacations abroad to such exotic places as Majorca. Many Wellingtonians, however, preferred to take holidays in Britain, often in the form of coach tours and breaks at seaside resorts, staying at B&Bs or holiday camps. Cawthorne's jewellery shop is to the right of the turning that leads to the Charlton Arms hotel car park. Copyright Abbeycolor.

Aston & Son's main furniture and carpet showroom in New Street, with the Wesleyan Methodist church and entrance to The Majestic ballroom to the left. Aston's more modern showroom stood a little further up on the opposite side of the road, immediately before Jack Ward's newsagents. Copyright Abbeycolor.

A section of New Street. From left to right: Smith's fishmongers, two cottages occupied by Albert Faulkner and Walter Rimmer, the Rendezvous Café (previously Jefferies' antiques, milliners and drapery stores) and a gardening supplies shop (formerly 'little' Espley's butchers) that had recently been acquired by the Co-operative Society. Copyright Abbeycolor.

Frank Sansom's distinctive house furnishings shop on the corner of Victoria Street (to the left) and New Street. The business transferred here from Market Street during the 1920s and at one time sold furniture made by ex-servicemen. It was demolished around 1970 to make way for the ring road. Copyright Abbeycolor.

Foundry Lane, which disappeared entirely when the ring road was constructed in the early 1970s. Former panification works were on the left; the old fire station and rear entrance to the swimming baths lay to the right.

Church Street seen from Market Square. The pathway to the Morris Hall, which was the Labour Party headquarters and venue for many political and social events, is on the left immediately after the railway bridge, followed by Barber & Son estate agents, Stewart's baby products and toy shop, Richard Parkes' wine and spirit merchants, Steventon's outfitters, Lloyds Bank, Valeting Services, Agnew's outfitters and the Journal offices. Steps up to the Lych Gate (dedicated in 1922) and All Saints parish church garden of rest are to the right. Copyright Abbeycolor.

Bridge Road, with entrances to Gough's coal depot and the railway sidings to the left. John Bromley's agricultural engineering and farm machinery depot is on the right and Hall, Wateridge & Owen's estate agents is on the extreme right before the corner into Market Street. Copyright Abbeycolor.

Upper New Street. From the left: the entrance to the temporary car park by the Wesleyan Methodist church, The Majestic ballroom, Aston's showroom, Beard's butchers and Florence Dixon's ladies' fashions. The Co-operative Society's (formerly Greenfield's) music depot is on the corner of Victoria Street opposite Sansom's furniture shop. Copyright Abbeycolor.

Herbert Jones stands in the doorway to his house (which was once one of Tom Austin's newspaper shops), next door to Frank Tinsley's fruit and grocery shop. Briscoe's hardware store is just visible on the extreme right. Copyright Abbeycolor.

The top end of New Street. Part of the Three Crowns public house is on the left followed by cottages occupied by George Johnson, Cecil Herring (formerly a general store) and the Hitchin family. John Giles' general stores is immediately before the opening into Chapel Lane with Avery Scales (and the van) on the other side. The Giles family kept a squealing monkey in their back yard and a squawking parrot in the house. Copyright Abbeycolor.

The western end of Foundry Road viewed from Union Road, which led to the Wrekin Hospital. The road running across the picture from right to left is Wrekin Road. A row of old cottages had already been demolished to create a temporary car park, in readiness for the creation of the ring road. The property behind the wall on the left was the Urban District Council services yard.

Upper High Street. On the right-hand side, from left to right: the Hand and Heart public house, with Alf Davies' family home next door, then Wilkinson's, followed by Roma's delicatessen (formerly Purcell's grocery). The property on the extreme right (on the corner of New Church Road) was, until around 1930, the Red Lion public house run by John Corbett. The King's Head can just be seen at the far end on the left side of the road. Copyright Abbeycolor.

For All Music . . .

FIELD'S at YOUR Service

- SHEET MUSIC
- GRAMOPHONE RECORDS
  (H.M.V., Columbia, Parlophone, Decca, Brunswick, Capitol, etc.)
- RECORD CASES and ALBUMS
- NEEDLES and STRINGS

WE EXCHANGE AND SELL RECORD TOKENS

Telephone
839

STATION ROAD
WELLINGTON

Left: Florence Roberts' high-quality women's and children's clothing shop (formerly Singer Sewing Machines) and the third of Espley's butchers shops in New Street, this one selling beef as opposed to pork. Copyright Abbeycolor. Right: Advertisement for Field's music depot in Station Road (next to the Midland Bank), which catered for musicians and music enthusiasts. Although 16s, 33s and 45s (both single and extended play) vinyl records were the norm, Field's were still supplying heavy carbon 78s at this time. E.W. Jones Electrical in New Street was gradually superseding Field's in record sales, probably because they sold hi-fi systems and had pegboard-sided hardboard 'listening booths' (rather like telephone booths) fixed to the walls of their upstairs record department.

Left: Church Street, with Barber & Son estate agents next door to Stewart's, which stocked virtually everything (especially prams and baby linen) for mothers-to-be, as well as a fine range of toys manufactured by companies such as Brittain's. Richard Parkes' wines and spirits (The Bacchus) is on the right. Right: Samuel Harold Tranter's surgical and bespoke boot and shoe maker's shop at 78 New Street. Samuel had occupied the premises from the 1920s and by 1960 he was close to retirement. The shop was demolished around 1962. Both photographs copyright Abbeycolor.

Twelve
Entertainment

Wellington was never short of entertainments. It had clubs, societies, cinemas and dance halls. Television was still in its infancy and did not have the same hold on people's attention as it has today. Radio, which was much more popular, enabled folk to get on with their hobbies and chores without demanding visual attention. In short, people preferred to do things to amuse themselves, rather than slump stupefied in front of a box for hours on end. To amuse oneself required energy, willpower, conscious thought and a willingness to meet fellow citizens, whatever their background and social standing.

Entertainments did not necessarily involve spending vast sums of money, which was just as well because most people did not have an abundance of it. Furthermore, because 'buy now, pay later' credit facilities did not exist, folk were a little more careful about how and when they spent their hard-earned cash.

The range of leisure pursuits available in Wellington in 1960 was wide. There was something to please everyone. Cinema attendance was particularly high; the usual pattern was for one programme to run from Monday to Wednesday, another from Thursday to Saturday and 'restricted' (X-rated) films presented to godless heathens on Sundays. A programme rarely

The Clifton cinema in Bridge Road, where 'Two Way Stretch' featuring Peter Sellers is showing. The building on the right was used for a while by the Wrekin Brewery Ltd as a bottling plant. The Clifton opened in January 1937 and staged concerts, operas and variety shows as well as movies. Copyright Abbeycolor.

consisted of just one film – it was normal to have a 'short' (possibly a Disney-style documentary or cartoon), a 'B' movie (which was seldom worth the celluloid it was printed on) and finally the main feature. Pathe Pictorial newsreels and an array of badly-made advertisements for local businesses helped to fill in the gaps (intervals) while usherettes purveyed ice creams, lollies and cigarettes from trays supported by straps around their necks. Kia Ora orange drinks came in cardboard cartons with paper straws designed to disintegrate after five seconds. But it was fun. And it was surprising how quickly the auditorium could empty during the final credits before the national anthem concluded the last performance.

Wellington had three cinemas at that time. The oldest was the Grand Theatre in Tan Bank. The Clifton in Bridge Road had opened in 1937 and was much larger, even having an upstairs seating area where admission costs were higher but courting couples were afforded some privacy. The town hall in Market Street also showed movies and, unlike the Grand and Clifton, had something of a reputation (justifiably) for being the local flea-pit. It had certainly had its day, and seldom advertised in the local papers, yet still managed to attract an audience.

The Clifton provided a much-appreciated service on Saturday mornings when it opened its doors for the Children's Saturday Club. For a modest sixpence, children tore noisily through the doors into the downstairs auditorium to watch cartoons, yesteryear comedy films starring *The Three Stooges* and serialized versions of *Batman* and *Zorro* which always ended with an American voiceover yelling 'Will our hero escape in time?' and exhorting everyone to come back next week. Which they did. Without fail. And they sold raspberry-flavoured penny ice lollies.

A popular alternative to the cinema was going to a dance. If it was Saturday night, The Majestic ballroom was the place to go, unless you belonged to one of the town's youth clubs. The Majestic had live bands and sold alcoholic drinks. It was the only place holding weekly dances until Terry Heath opened his Town House in 1960, a development that benefitted the public by provoking competition and thereby encouraging higher standards. In time, the battle for attendances would be won by the Town House, but for the moment both flourished. Dance-

The Grand Theatre, 'the cosiest cinema in town', in Tan Bank, which at the time was showing Rock Hudson and Doris Day in 'Pillow Talk'. The building was originally an American roller-skating rink and became the Rink Picture Palace in 1911; in 1912 it changed its name to the Grand Theatre. Copyright Abbeycolor.

The town hall, venue of many dinners and dances as well as the town's third cinema. A veritable flea pit in the customary sense, it rarely advertised performances and closed during 1960 when it became a 'pop in' club for teenagers. A.E. Giles' sweets and tobacco store, which also acted as wholesale supplier in the town, is on the left, next to the entrance to Patterson's salerooms where frequent auctions were held. Mr Webb's seed and garden supplies store is on the right, one of several shops fronting the Market Hall. Copyright Abbeycolor.

The Majestic ballroom, known until the late 1930s as the Palais de Dance. Until 1960 this was the main provider of dinner-dance entertainment in the town. Saturday night dances were extremely popular and an excellent place to meet members of the opposite sex. Various bands provided the music. Copyright Abbeycolor.

Saturday night at The Majestic. From left to right: Joan Meyrick, John Horler, Helen Horler, Don Wood, Bert Wedge, Rose Evans, Trevor Hawkins, Marjorie Hawkins. Men were expected to wear formal suits and ties (pullovers were optional) and women suitable dance attire.

A scene from one of the Methodist youth club's Saturday night 'socials' inside the main Institute building (an ex-army wooden hut acquired from Cannock Chase in 1920), where club and church members and their friends enjoyed playing games as well as dancing. Music was provided by an old record player, the needle of which had a tendency to skip.

goers soon made their choice and stuck with their favoured venue. The Town House aspired to a better class of customer, better dressed and better behaved. The Majestic, true to its origins, catered for everyone without pretension. Signs of how the two evolved became more noticeable towards the end of the 1960s when the Town House favoured discotheques rather than live performances by young hopefuls.

Other dances were put on by youth clubs for their own members and friends. Only soft drinks were generally available (although it was not unknown for people to nip out for a 'proper' drink before returning) but that suited organizational rules; you could probably have more fun remaining sober. Regular dances, called 'socials', were arranged at New Street Methodist church, sometimes just for members of the youth club but at other times thrown open to everyone. As well as dancing to all styles of music (from pop to ballroom; many teenagers would attempt the slow waltz just to smooch around the French-chalked timber dancefloor) played on a gramophone that rested on springs to reduce bounce, the evening was broken with group party games like Coach & Horses and who-can-lie-on-the-floor-smoking-a-cigarette-and-make-the-longest-tower-of-ash-before-it-falls-off. There was always, of course, an interval for refreshments. Pop supplied by O.D. Murphy's works on Holyhead Road was always popular.

Dinner dances arranged by employers and sports clubs (as well as wedding receptions) in the vicinity were another means of entertainment. The main venues in 1960 were the Forest Glen by the Wrekin Hill, and The Majestic, The Town House and the Charlton Arms in Wellington itself. Hotels such as the Red Lion and the Falcon on Holyhead Road catered very well for smaller groups.

The Young Men's Christian Association (YMCA) provided a wide range of activities for its members (who were both male and female) and their friends, including a snack bar open twelve hours a day. It celebrated its 100th birthday in 1959 after having originally met at the Wesleyan Methodist chapel in New Street, which subsequently became the Chad Valley Wrekin Toy Works. Wellington Youth Club, another venture where indoor games like table tennis and various outdoor pursuits were organized, met in the evenings at Constitution Hill School.

Bar staff at the newly-opened Terry Heath's Town House, from left to right: -?-, Les Mincher, Reg Mansell, Bill Onions, Andrew Paterson. The Town House rapidly became a competitive alternative to The Majestic and played host to various well-known bands and national celebrities like Humphrey Littleton. The discos of the late 1960s were unforgettable, especially when the 'Go-Go Dancers' from BBC's Top of the Pops turned up.

Possibly the first dinner-dance to take place at The Town House: here the Wellington Nursing Division celebrates its twenty-first anniversary on Friday 17 June 1960.

The executive committee of the YMCA. Clockwise around the table, from front centre-right: H. Chaplin, J. Tipping, W. Jenkins, T. Haden, T. Anslow, E. Mosdell, H.N. Lightbown (secretary), T.C. Buttrey, MBE (chairman), W.J. Laud (vice-chairman), W.G. Newman, T.W. Pollard, R. Pritchard. Many were businessmen in the town. Mr Buttrey was headmaster at Prince's Street Junior School. The YMCA celebrated its hundredth anniversary in 1959 when this photograph was taken.

There were also numerous church organizations, many raising funds from Saturday coffee mornings, which arranged various spiritual and social meetings at different times during the week. All ages were catered for and, although attendance at the relevant church was desirable, it was seldom a prerequisite of membership. This was particularly true of Sunday schools, which were still very well attended at this time, even to the point where children willingly took examinations, which were sponsored by the Bible Reading Society and held in the YMCA building. There was much to do, plenty to get involved with... and very little trouble or vandalism. Leisure time could be spent well if you had the inclination, and many folk had.

The most flourishing youth club, attracting a high degree of loyalty from its members, was that run by New Street Methodist church. Its origins can be traced back to September 1943; by the mid-1950s it offered a wide range of activities, including social responsibility efforts like gardening for the elderly. Many of its members also joined the church itself and met after the Sunday evening service for discussions and semi-devotional gatherings at someone's house, usually club leader Ken Jones' house at Bridge End, Orleton Lane. On the whole it was an outgoing club, often liaising with other youth groups in the town as well as societies within its own church group. Evening 'mystery' trips, plays, reviews, pantomimes, debates, scavenger hunts, sports (where enthusiasm was seldom matched by results) like rounders, table tennis, darts and football, craft classes, social evenings and dances were regular features of club life. It was a place where teenagers from all walks of life came to have fun in free surroundings without being preached at or put under undue pressure to change their lives. Not surprisingly, attendance resulted in many marriages.

Two activities in particular caused an immense amount of anticipation. The first was the annual club holiday, which usually entailed hiring a school at a seaside resort and a coach from one of the local coach operators. For a very modest price and a lot of (shared) hard work, members were able to spend August Bank Holiday week (at that time the first week in the month that happened to coincide with one of Sankey's main holiday weeks) away from their

The New Street Methodist youth club on one of their regular rambles, this one on Easter Monday 1960. The club was extremely well supported with a loyal membership who took part in a wide variety of events throughout the year. It was probably the most successful youth club the town has ever seen. It began as a social club in September 1943, when membership was free to armed forces personnel, and continued until the early 1970s.

parents but under the watchful eye of several adult organizers and helpers. It gave them the opportunity to see sights and take part in various pursuits. Even so long after the end of the Second World War, it was still uncommon for families to holiday very far from home unless it was to visit relatives elsewhere in Britain, or to spend a day at the seaside on an excursion provided by railway or coach companies. Club holidays were an excellent adventure.

The second event was the annual club pantomime, which took place in early December and sometimes coincided with a fair held on the rough car park in front of Belmont Hall. The standard of performance was invariably high (despite missed cues, fluffed lines and props doing their own thing) – so much so that people flocked from all over the area to attend. Once the choice of pantomime had been made, cast members and helpers threw themselves into the project from September onwards. Almost everyone in the club contributed something towards ensuring its success. The Institute, with its small stage, constituted the theatre and, in spite of it being constructed entirely of aging timber, always managed to pass safety tests carried out by

Members of New Street Methodist youth club on their annual holiday, this one at Whippingham, Isle of Wight. Back row, from left to right: Ron Poulter, Dave Frost, Godfrey Harrison, David Davies, Ken Poulter, John Parton, Ian Donaldson, Ron George (bus driver), Jim Wiley, Dave 'Daz' Beechey. Second row from back: Dave Grindley, Neville Archer, Allan Frost, Brian Donaldson (signwriter), Charlie 'Wakey-wakey' Gale, Ken Jones (club leader), Colin Lane, Roger Parton. Second row from front, seated: Les Frost ('official' photographer), Edward Wakeley, Brian Picken, Margaret Jones, Mary Frost, Margaret Edwards, Marion Butler, Lesley Holmes, Ida Jones, Wendy Hancox, Mrs Cheverton (Whippingham School cook, hired for the week), Wendy Lovatt, Bert Butler, Jennifer Pearce, Margaret Frost, Marion Dolby, Wendy Newnes. Front row: Alan Jones, Mary Butler, Kay Hullin, Vivien Taylor, Joyce Cotton, Mary Fletcher, Joan Petford. The holiday would take place in August Bank Holiday week and members saved throughout the year to pay the £7 10s it cost to go. Wherever possible, the club hired a school and its facilities in or near a coastal resort, and operated a rota system for members to prepare food, wash up, clean toilets etc. The sexes were strictly separated at night, each having their own classroom dormitory where they slept on the club's camp beds and lilos. One of the local bus companies (on this occasion it was George Cooper's of Oakengates) provided both coach and driver to take the group to and from their destination, as well as on several excursions during the week. Without these arrangements, many members simply would not have had a holiday away from home. While there, the club played host to German teenagers also on holiday in the area.

Wellington fire brigade. A smaller second hut, comprising two Sunday school rooms linked via a covered walkway to the main building, provided changing rooms for male and female performers. The 'panto' was an event not to be missed.

Churches in the town occasionally held joint services, usually to mark special events that were observed by everyone, regardless of sect or creed. However, social activities were, as a rule, kept separate. Like now, almost every venture relied heavily on volunteer help to advertise, supervise or provide those inevitable but welcome refreshments. Every organization had its own small army of stalwarts who not only gave up their time but also often made or supplied provisions at their own expense. They were invaluable and could, in their own small but crucial way, ensure an event's success. Furthermore, over the years they developed an uncanny skill for knowing just how much food to provide so that none went to waste, and they knew how to get the best out of antiquated equipment, such as tea urns and ancient gas cookers.

Summer garden parties (held at the homes of church members), autumn 'bazaars' (in church

The New Street Methodist youth club's annual pantomime was always high on the list of must-see entertainments in Wellington. The 1960 production, using a script suitably adapted by Samuel French to give jokes a local flavour, was 'Aladdin'. Muriel Bishop painted the scenery, assisted by Audrey Shuker; Les Frost made the props with the help of George Miles, Charlie Gale and Alan Jones. Lighting and other effects were created by Laurie Marsh (the librarian at Wellington library), Neville Archer, Jim Wiley and Dave Moore. Ken Jones provided piano accompaniment and costumes were hired from a theatrical agency, though there were also some made by members of the club and church. The producers of this production, the fourteenth put on by the club according to the Wellington Journal, were Mary Fletcher and Ida and Ken Jones. The leading actors were Mary Fletcher (Aladdin), Brian Donaldson (Abanazar), Ken Roberts (Widow Twankey), Marion Dolby (Hoo Sit), Pat Danks (Princess Jenin), Kay Hullin (Abdul), Edward Wakeley (Mustapha Biyeh), Vivien Taylor (Slave of the Ring), Wendy Hancox (Slave of the Lamp), Wendy Newnes (Princess's Maid), Roger Parton (Sultan), Colin Lane (Court Chamberlain), Ian Donaldson (Demon). The chorus was comprised of Mary Butler, Linda Cole, Claudette Russell, Gill Edwards, Wendy Lovatt, Beryl Donaldson, Carol Tracey, Veronica Woolliscroft, Hilary Carline, Janet Burden, Margaret Edwards, Margaret Jones, Joan Petford and Edna Grattidge. Beryl Davies, Jacqueline Bennett, Jennifer Scott, Gillian Bennett, Dianne Newnes, Dylis Stokes, Winifred Loynton and Ann Lewin were ballet dancers. Allan Frost played the (invisible) performing flea, hence cannot be seen.

halls) and highly popular 'rummage sales' (charity shops didn't exist then) were a few of the ways in which funds were raised. The former two encompassed a variety of entertainments: sales of hand-produced wares like knitted clothing, 'bran tubs' (sawdust-filled tubs containing wrapped toys for children to delve into to 'win' a prize), fake fortune-telling booths and the like. Rummage sales were wonderful places to pick up bargains and household goods, and useless articles like fox furs with an interestingly undefinable smell. Tending a stall was not for the faint hearted: a veritable stampede followed the opening of the doors and punters, who had earlier formed a long and orderly queue outside, rifled through rows of neatly laid-out goods, flinging items heavenwards in their search for bargains. Bartering was impossible; punters had their own ideas about what meagre amounts they were prepared to spend. Nevertheless, every penny (it certainly did not amount to pounds, or even florins) counted.

Churches were also important venues for other organizations – as well as youth clubs – committed to giving children of various age groups something worthwhile to do. Cubs, Brownies, Scouts and Guides were all run under the auspices of a church. The Boys' Brigade was run by Tan Bank Methodist Church. The Brigade was especially noted for its small band, which processed around the town centre streets on the first Sunday of each month before arriving back at the church, whereupon the monthly Family Service began.

Other leisure pursuits (as opposed to sporting activities) were organized by businesses and groups of individuals with a shared interest, such as photography. Margaret Kendrick's School of Dance gave ballroom dancing lessons as well as running a ballet class (normally for girls but occasionally for budding Rudolf Nureyevs) on Saturday mornings. Schools also had a multiplicity of end-of-day clubs and societies and depended very heavily on the goodwill, enthusiasm and commitment of their teaching staff.

Private music lessons were provided by a number of people: Gladys Evans and Irene Jarman in King Street, Mr S. Field (who owned the record shop in Station Road), Eric Latham in

Like other churches, New Street Methodist church held an annual garden party. The 1960 event was held at Ken and Monica Corbett's home in Leegomery Road. Here an audience watches a marionette petite puppet show performed by John Giles. John lived with his parents at their general store in New Street: his mother made the puppets' costumes (she was a dressmaker by trade) and he pre-recorded the entire soundtrack for the show on a Grundig reel-to-reel tape recorder. The remnants of a typical home-made go-cart lie to the left of the theatre.

Behind every successful church event lies a dedicated team preparing refreshments. On this occasion, (from left to right) Nellie Breakwell, Ida Jones, Mrs Jukes, Mary Frost, Marion Butler, Agnes Morris and Phyllis Taylor are at work in the cramped kitchen at New Street Methodist Church Institute. The Institute was home to virtually every church event and was occasionally rented out to other organizations. Even the Chad Valley factory made use of it during the Second World War to make goods for the armed services.

Tan Bank Methodist Church ran the highly successful 1st Wellington Company of the Boys' Brigade. Among the boys seen here forming the guard of honour at the October 1960 wedding of Lieutenants Derek Whittingham and Irene Eccleshall are Roy Grimwood, Geoffrey Lloyd, Peter Hadfield, Bernard Waters, Kelvin McLeod, David Vaughan and Michael Wilkinson.

Holyhead Road, Florence Wilkins in Golf Links Lane and, perhaps most notably, Edith Walton in Mill Bank were between them able to tutor pupils of all ages in singing and playing a remarkable range of musical instruments.

One of the most widely enjoyed events took place every Whit Saturday – the town carnival. Countless businesses and organizations spent small fortunes decorating themed floats and joined a long procession led by army and other bands, and dance troups, around the streets before finishing up at the Buck's Head football ground, where a funfair, games and other attractions kept the crowds happy until late into the night. The annual carnival raised quite considerable sums to benefit the council chairman's chosen charity. It was also an event for which the whole town pulled together.

On the domestic front, televisions provided a range of programmes to suit all the family. While standards may be rather primitive compared to today's, the overall quality was high and unlikely to cause offence to any viewer. One main difference was that people were prepared to listen. Dialogue and a good plot were more important than visual effects; those were the province of the cinema. Radio shows featuring talks, drama, news broadcasts and music were still more widely enjoyed than television (although the *Range Rider, Cisco Kid, William Tell, Lone Ranger, Picture Book, Andy Pandy, Bill and Ben, Rag, Tag and Bobtail* and *The Woodentops* amused children while *The Black and White Minstrel Show* and *Sunday Night at the London Palladium* entertained adults).

'Going up' from Cubs to Scouts. One of the cubs who 'went up' on this occasion was John Woolley (front row, third from the right). Among the scouts and officers pictured here are 'Smudge' Smith, Peter Brayne, Henry Purcell, John Munt, 'Tad' Adams, John Richards, Tony Burrows, Chris Fabish, Bernard Bagnall, Allan Payne, Mick Clay, John Pardoe, ? Burrows, John Burrows, Roger Eccleston, John Osborne, Allan Minton, Roger Tipton, Cathy Dean, Cedric Ayres, Brendan Forsyth, Dave Bevis, Alistair Ayres, Mary Osborne and John Treherne. The group met at the Scout Hut on Church Walk alongside All Saints parish church.

A Saturday morning class of ballet hopefuls at the Margaret Kendrick School of Dance. Among those posing in this group are Susan Robinson (back row, far right), Elizabeth Paterson (front row, far left), Susan Osleton (front row, third from right) and Fiona Robinson (front row, far right).

The Wizard of Oz float by the Wrekin Hospital in the town's annual carnival in June 1960. From left to right: Elizabeth Paterson (Lion), Sister Lee (Tin Man) and her son (Bird), Sister Elsie Paterson (Scarecrow), -?- (Wizard), Sylvia Caswell (Dorothy).

HOBSON & Co.

(STATIONERS) LTD.

Printers and Manufacturing
Stationers

Picture Framers and
Fancy Goods Dealers

MARKET SQUARE

Phone : Wellington 54

G. W. HARVEY

Jeweller
and Silversmith

4 MARKET STREET
WELLINGTON

Established 1860
TELEPHONE : 352

WREKIN CARRIERS, LTD.

Suppliers of Sand and Gravel for Concrete
Gravel or Red Shale for paths and drives
Building Sand, Ashes and Hardcore
Excavators and Tipping Lorries for hire

HADLEY ROAD - LEEGOMERY - Nr. WELLINGTON

Phone : WELLINGTON 1161/2

MONDAY, 9th MAY, 1960   **SHREWSBURY**   Kick-Off 6.30 p.m.

SHREWSBURY

1
Miller

2   3
Hobson   Skeech

4   5   6
Harley   Wallace   Walters

7   8   10   11
Ireland   Starkey   Ambler or Edgley   Rowley   Whitaker

Referee—   Linesmen—

J. Griffiths (Shrop. County F.A.)   (Orange Flag)—J. S. Constable
                                     (Cerise Flag)—D. A. Griffiths

Snape   Griffiths   Cocum   Hurdley   Windsor
11   10   9   8   7
Davies G.   Davies N   Manders
6   5   4
Rodgers   Whitehouse
3   2
                    Richards
Colours—Black & White   1   WELLINGTON TOWN

ANY ALTERATIONS WILL BE ANNOUNCED OVER LOUD SPEAKER

HEATHS

Restaurant
and
Coffee Bar

IN
New Street
IS OPEN
BEFORE & AFTER
THE MATCH
TO-DAY

Service and Quality

PRIVATE PARTIES TO
YOUR ORDER
OPEN TO 9 p.m.

An extract from a Wellington Town Football Club programme on the occasion of the local derby match against Shrewsbury Town.

Wellington Town Football Club, 1959/60 season at the Buck's Head ground on Watling Street. From left to right, back row: Joe Edwards, Doug Cooper, Gordon Pearce (vice chairman), Peter Brisbourne (treasurer), Les Saxton (secretary), Len Rigby. Middle row: Jim Kerr, Ron Manders, Neville Davies, Mick Richards, Gordon Davies (formerly of Wolverhampton Wanderers), G. Hoof, Bert Richards. Front row: Frank Naggington (chairman, standing), Bobby Windsor, Alwyn Rodgers (formerly of Doncaster Rovers and player of the year in 1960), Roy Pearce, Billy Hurdley, Johnny Hancocks (player-manager who left in December 1959 to be succeeded by Ron Lewin in April 1960).

Thirteen

Sport

Wellington hosted a number of sporting activities for anyone active enough to participate, and there was always plenty of opportunity to spectate. Unlike today, professional sportsmen were very much in the minority; because of this simple fact, admission prices were moderate and affordable, club strips lasted several years and support from fans could be extremely loyal, irrespective of performance or result. Facilities at even the most popular venues were limited, to say the least, but that did not prevent ardent supporters from turning out whatever the weather.

Wellington Town Football Club was still known as 'The Lilywhites' even though the team now wore black (as opposed to their former white) shorts. Then, as now, the stadium was never exactly packed during home games, a fact noted by the chairman and local press alike. Nor did the club have its own supporters' clubhouse; that would have to wait for the time being. Nevertheless, the club had ambition, at this time focused on the provision of floodlights to enable evening matches to be played. The Supporters' Club had several branches (including at Dawley and Lawley Bank) in 1960; everyone pulled together to raise the necessary cash, even

T. H. ROBERTS

(Proprietor : A. D. DRAKE)

for

SCOUT CLOTHING & EQUIPMENT

of all kinds

★

TRAVELLING REQUISITES

TRUNKS - SUIT CASES

ATTACHE CASES

SPORTS GOODS - GIFTS

FANCY LEATHER GOODS

GAMES

CAMPING EQUIPMENT

★

FIRST-CLASS REPAIRS TO ALL LEATHER

GOODS AND SPORTS EQUIPMENT

MARKET STREET

WELLINGTON

Telephone 541

Roberts' shop in Market Street, the main store for sporting goods. Photograph copyright Abbeycolor.

Wellington Hornets Rugby Union Football Club at their Admaston Road ground. From left to right, back row: M. Haylett, S. Needes, D. Hopkins, C. Gower, R. Shaw, J. Edmundson, B. Stanley. Middle row: K. Guy, R. Watkins, D. Owens, J. Bromley, M. Gwynne. Front row: P. Bromley, A. Wilson, R. Coward. They lost their first match, against Gwyn Bayliss' XV in September, 6-38. Some 200 people turned up to support them.

Wellington Cricket Club 1st XI at the ground off Haygate Road. From left to right, back row: D. Lee, D. Rogers, R. Machin, R. Heighway, T. Deakin, J. Westwood, B. Davies, Mr. Hall, Mr. Bourne. Front row: J. Holding, P. Fletcher, C. Wakeley (captain), W. Dumbell, C. Evans.

to the point of holding a dance at the Majestic in March. It would be several more years before floodlights were installed.

The team came a disappointing seventeenth in the Southern League Premier Division (out of twenty-two clubs) in the 1959/60 season, and eighth in 1960/61. The fact that the team was comprised of part-time players may have contributed to their somewhat inconsistent level of performance.

1960 saw the first games played by Wellington Hornets Rugby Union Football Club, at a ground acquired in Admaston Road. The team had, until this time, been based at and sponsored by Joseph Sankey & Sons at their Hadley Castle engineering works.

The ground of the town's cricket club has been off Haygate Road since the year after the club's formation in 1946 (its first chairman was Ken Corbett). The ground was generously given to the club by Col. Herbert, later Earl of Powis, and was formerly part of his Orleton Park estate. The Earl became president of the cricket club in 1948 and died in 2001. The ground is in a wonderful location, with The Wrekin Hill providing an impressive backdrop.

Golf at Wellington was originally played on links belonging to Wellington (later renamed Wrekin) College towards the end of the nineteenth century. The sport acquired its present location when Wrekin Golf Club was founded in 1905. As with other golf clubs, there were very strict rules governing membership, appearance and etiquette. In keeping with the times,

Wrekin Golf Club when the first Long and Short competition was played. From left to right: Dennis Boyle (nine times club champion), ? Atkinson (club professional and steward), Geoff Locke, Frank Bayley, Jim Espley, Tony Espley, ? Williams (scratch golfer based at Central Ordnance Depot, Donnington), Walter Espley (club president), Tom Owen, Colin Espley, Pat Stroud (secretary and treasurer). The club, formed in 1905, was once described in a guide as being only ten minutes' walk from Wellington railway station: people must either have had longer legs or been much fitter in those days! The original clubhouse, pictured here, was situated a few metres south of the boys' grammar school and was later demolished to make way for the M54 motorway. The present clubhouse, built at the end of an extension to Golf Links Lane, was to be officially opened in October 1972. The course has long been acknowledged as one of the most picturesque in Britain.

Wellington Swimming Baths, built in 1910 and demolished in 1980.

Annual prize giving at Wellington Swimming Club. From left to right, back row: Joan Bonsall, Roger Tonks, Bert Wedge, Viv Lees, Dave Moore, Kathy ?, -?-, Brian Medley, Joyce Dixon, -?-, Jane Bayley, Brian Ward, Angela Jones, Anthony Toogood. Middle row: Susan McGowan, -?-, -?-, -?-, Mrs Wiseman (Councillor Wiseman's wife, presenting the prizes), Jonathon Dawson, -?-, -?-. Front row: Sid Price, -?-, Tessa Magness, Moira (?) Hughes, Gwen Crittenden, Maggie Maughan, Ann Maughan, Delyth (?) Jones, Lynette Fisher-Jones, Alan Wales.

policies have relaxed somewhat in more recent years. The original clubhouse had to be relocated when the M54 motorway cut through the northern slopes of the Ercall Hill.

Swimming has been one of the most popular sports in the town since the first public baths were constructed in 1910. It had been a long time coming; the first proposals were mooted during the mid-1800s. Until the baths were built, swimmers had been obliged to venture into the unsafe waters of the town's reservoirs in Ercall Wood and at the foot of the Wrekin, and even in the river Severn.

Bowls (Crown Green rather than ten-pin, which tended to be played between bales of straw at garden fêtes) was largely confined to older players, but younger members were already making their mark on greens at the Charlton Arms Hotel and Bowring Recreation Ground. Tennis was also catered for, with small but loyal lawngoers playing during the summer months near Wrekin College and Christ Church.

Snooker was provided for at the billiards hall in Tan Bank. The game was, at this time, not considered suitable for impressionable youngsters, whose parents discouraged visits to the hall.

Sporting activities were not confined to official bodies. The town's youth clubs (including the YMCA) not only provided a range of indoor games (such as table tennis, darts, etc.) but also fielded teams to play against other youth clubs and social clubs sponsored by long-established engineering companies (Sankey's, Glynwed, Maddock's, etc.) in the area.

While football was perhaps the most prolific (many boys grew up playing football in the streets and play areas so understood the rudiments of the game, even to the point of knowing when the 'ref' had to be shot or given a new pair of spectacles), netball, rounders, tennis, cricket and the relatively new sport of badminton were also very popular. Supporters were, in the main, other club members and their girl- or boyfriends. As with all amateur matches, taking part in the game and upholding a club's good name was just as important as the result. It had to be:

New Street Methodist youth club 1st (and only) XI football team, 1960/61 season, at Bowring Recreation Ground. From left to right, back row: Alan Poulter, Colin Lane, Vic Griffiths, Ken Poulter, John Childs, Dave Moore, Edward Wakeley (trainer). Front row: Tony Picken, Wally Harper, Don Weston, Brian Lowe, Bob Parton. Memories are vague but it is believed that the team may have won one match in three seasons.

PROGRAMME		SECTIONS & LEADERS	
		Art	Birmingham University, Extra Mural Dept.
MONDAY	Table Tennis Match. Boys' Club	Athletics	M. Head
	Judo (Men, Women). Choir	Angling	R. Pessall
		Badminton	G. Page
TUESDAY	Basketball. Football Cl. (1st Tues.)	Basketball	E. Rigby
	Whist Drive. Ladies' Club	Billiards & Snooker	D. K. Tipping
	Extra Mural Lectures	Boys' Work	R. Pritchard
		British Boys for British Farms	General Secretary
WEDNESDAY	Judo (Men, Women). Films	Camping and Holidays at Home and Abroad	P. E. Hookway
	W.E.A. Women's Hour	Centennial History	T. W. Pollard
		Chess	D. B. Holland
THURSDAY	Training Night · Snooker Practice	Choir	D. H. Hallifax
	Committees	Cricket	
		Drama	Mrs. M. Roberts
FRIDAY	Badminton (Senior, Boys)	Films	J. D. Hamilton
	Junior Boys' Club. Snooker Match	Football	D. K. Tipping
	Chess. T.T. Practice	Judo—Men	J. B. Evanson
		Women	Miss A. Jones
SATURDAY	Football. Dance (as arranged)	Ladies' Club	Miss D. Ward
	Judo	Lawn Tennis	B. Tudor
		Members' Council	E. Mosdell, W. Jenkins
SUNDAY	Sunday Club, 3 p.m.	Olde Tyme Dance	E. Mosdell
		Overseas Work	
Daily—Lounge, Snack Bar Service (9.30 a.m. to 9.30 p.m.), Radio, Newspapers, Billiards and Snooker, Table Tennis, Table Games, etc.		Sea Training	General Secretary
		Snack Bar	T. W. Pollard
		Sunday Club	E. Mosdell, R. Pritchard
		Table Tennis—Seniors	
		Juniors	B. Griffiths
Football Ground—Bennett's Bank, Holyhead Road junction of Haybridge Road.		Whist Drives	E. Haden
		Women's Hour	Mrs. V. Smith
		Women's Auxiliary	Mrs. A. Johnson

Where there is a blank in place of a name, inquiries to the General Secretary, but a *volunteer* is wanted.

The programme of regular events and list of section leaders at the YMCA.

Wellington Boys Grammar School badminton team. From left to right, back row: Geoff Cubbin, John Phillips, Roger Davies, John Burrows. Front row: Michael Lunn, Peter Byram.

disappointment is a way of life to casual sportsmen and women. Occasional victories taste that much sweeter and can be remembered, relived and talked about for a long time afterwards.

Schools played a valuable part in the promotion of sporting events. Every capable pupil was legally obliged to participate in some form of physical activity every week during the academic year. Not only did classmates play against each other during games afternoons, but the better players were expected to uphold the school's reputation at matches played on Saturday mornings against other schools and, occasionally, sporting clubs like Wellington Cricket Club. Rugby Union football was almost totally confined to the boys grammar school and Wrekin College (many excellent needle-matches took place between them over the years), although occasional games were played against teams fielded by secondary modern schools in the district. Strangely enough, parents were seldom seen supporting their child's team at away or even home matches.

Every school in the town held a summer sports day. Parents, usually mothers, much to their children's embarrassment, were actively encouraged to witness these long, drawn-out proceedings. Almost every child took part; the less sporty might be entered in egg-and-spoon, three-legged, sack and slow bicycle races, whereas the more active took part in track and field events. Most schools ran a 'house' system to encourage competition. In 1960, for example, Park Junior School divided pupils into four houses named after notable Shropshire celebrities (Clive, Hunt, Stretton and Webb) while the boys grammar school had three (named after local hills Wrekin, Ercall and Lawrence – Maddocks was added a few years later). Houses at the secondary modern school were Sidney, Benbow, Clive and Darwin. A colour (red, green, yellow or blue) represented each house to help spectators cheer on the right team. To promote competition still further, schools were expected to enter teams in Shropshire Schools and Wrekin Area athletics events held annually on the playing fields of one of the larger schools.

SHROPSHIRE EDUCATION COMMITTEE

FLOREAT SALOPIA

ATHLETICS CERTIFICATE

AWARDED TO

Name A. Frost

School Park Junior,

Event 80 yds   - 1st.

Date 30th. June 1960.

Shropshire Education Committee provided a range of sport-related certificates for schools to complete and present to pupils who successfully participated in a number of events. They were considered a mark of achievement.

Wellington Boys Grammar School under-16 football team, 1959/60. From left to right, back row: Peter Byram, Geoff Millman, Mick Roberts, John Lewis, Geoff (?) Pike, Alan Lowndes. Front row: Alan Hughes, Brian Davies, Dave Pointon (captain), Les Lloyd, Colin Bayliss.

Wellington Boys Grammar School 1st XV rugby union football team, 1959/60. From left to right, back row: Ralph Edwards, Gerard Charlton, John Pardoe, Brian Earle, Michael Lunn, Robert Briscoe, Alan West, Ian Holloway, Ted Farthing. Middle row: Pete Reynolds, Neil Summerton, Bill Newbold, Dave Frost (captain), A.P. Anslow, Keith Edwards. Front row: Ron Harris, Mike Corfield, Peter Edwards, John Johnson.

Wellington Girls High School hockey team, 1960/61. From left to right, back row: Judy Bale, Sue MacGregor, Jane Dyas, Wendy Martin, Sue Attrill, Sue Pointon. Front row: Lilian Greenfield, Sybil Heath, Chris Taylor, Jennifer Morris, Margaret Pillar.

Wellington Girls High School senior rounders team, 1959/60. From left to right, back row: Gillian Edwards, Nicola Fermain, Sue Adams, Linda Hamps, Pauline Mabbott, Carol Tracey, Valerie Jones. Front row: Mary Butler, Pauline George, Vivien Taylor.

Mr R.H. Dahl came to Wellington as headmaster of Wrekin College in 1952. Under his leadership, musical and sporting activities flourished while at the same time the college's record of high academic achievement was maintained. He took pride in the fact that he knew every student by name.

A contemporary advertisement for St Chad's Preparatory School, which was, like Old Hall School on Holyhead Road, quite selective when deciding which pupils gained places. Such education did not come cheap, nor did the school have accommodation for many boarders. Consequently, the majority of children came from local homes with an upper middle-class background.

St. Chad's Preparatory School

(late " THE GROVE ")

PARK WALLS : WHITCHURCH ROAD
WELLINGTON   ::   ::   SALOP

- KINDERGARTEN AND PREPARATORY FOR BOYS AND GIRLS (5 to 14).
- PREPARATION FOR GRAMMAR SCHOOL AND COMMON ENTRANCE EXAMINATIONS TO PUBLIC SCHOOLS.
- RIDING TAUGHT——QUALIFIED STAFF.
- A FEW BOARDERS (Boys) TAKEN AT REASONABLE FEES.

Prospectus from : **REVD. A. M. DUTTON**, Headmaster

Telephone : WELLINGTON 295

114

Fourteen
Schooldays

Wellington schools in existence in 1960 were as follows.

Secondary: Boys Grammar in Golf Links Lane
                  Girls High in King Street
                  Secondary Modern (mixed) at Orleton Lane
                  St Patrick's Catholic School in Mill Bank
Primary: Barn Farm County Infants off Dawley Road
                  Constitution Hill County Infants
                  Orleton Lane County Infants
                  Prince's Street County Junior
                  St Patrick's Catholic School in North Road
                  Park County Junior, on North Road, with its annexe in Wrekin Road.
Private schools: St Chad's at Park Walls
                  Old Hall on Holyhead Road.

Wrekin College was the only public school whose pupils (all boys at the time), wearing grey jackets and black trousers, could be seen strolling around the town on Wednesday afternoons (half day closing for shops and virtually every other tempting enterprise) and Sunday mornings, on their way to one of the churches in the town.

Both Old Hall and St Chad's had excellent reputations as 'preparatory' schools; parents had to pay quite substantial sums for their children to attend, although a few aided places were available each year. Money, of course, does not buy intelligence or academic success but schools such as these were regarded as stepping-stones to a 'better' future.

Most children in the town attended one of the county schools. Standards varied, both academically and behaviourally. Infants' schools taught the rudiments of the three 'R's. Particular attention was given to multiplication tables (imprinted on the outside cover of exercise books), mental arithmetic and spelling. Music lessons took the form of coloured notes (a different colour for each child's percussion instrument; the teacher's piano provided the tune) written on staves on the blackboard. The result was truly cacophonous. Even the more gifted pupils might have to wait until junior school to learn how to play the recorder. Advanced instruments (piano, violin, trumpet, clarinet, etc.) were taught at secondary schools after the end of normal lessons and on Saturday mornings. Badly-behaved pupils could expect a sharp rap from a wooden ruler across the palm of the hand or back of the leg. 'Monitors' were responsible for filling inkwells, carrying third-of-a-pint bottles of milk in crates into each classroom, cleaning blackboards and even wooden-framed slates in the few schools where these were still found to be useful educational tools.

Differences in social class and academic ability became slightly more noticeable in the junior schools. Park Junior (where Ralph Brookes was headmaster) regarded itself as having the best facilities (it was, after all, the most modern in Wellington at that time); it also had a better success rate for children passing the eleven-plus examination to gain entry to the Boys Grammar or Girls High Schools. Furthermore, all pupils at Park were required to wear a

Wrekin Road Junior School. Mary Frost, pictured here with a group of children, was meals supervisor ('dinner lady') at the school for some twenty-five years. W.J. Laud's bakery and shop can be seen over the road amidst cottages which have now been demolished. Sidney Speed's popular sweet shop was located to the right of the photograph before the business moved to Laud's premises during the early 1960s.

1959 Barn Farm Infants School Christmas nativity play, 'The Living World Worships the Baby Jesus'. Taking part were Linda Plant (Mary), Joseph Oliver (Joseph), Julian Goode, Keith Williams and David Sherry (Shepherds), David Blythe, Paul Edwards and June Dalton (Kings), Ann Hammond, Betty Haycox, Marian Shepherd, Wendy Tanner, Andrew Sleeman, Sheila Luckock, Jocelyn Rogers, Alison Moore, Marilyn Sellers, Neville Dunn, Clive Carter, Julia Addison, Linda Carline, Clive Hillsley, Betty Powell, Susan Rennie and Susan Madeley.

uniform. If nothing else, school uniforms engendered a sense of equality and prevented parents from being harassed into cladding their offspring in overpriced 'fashionable' clothing.

Juniors were encouraged not only to learn essential academic subjects but also to participate in a wide variety of cultural events intended to widen their experience and knowledge. Children seldom rebelled; boys, for example, were given no choice but to take part in 'Music and Movement' lessons broadcast by BBC Radio or dance festivals organized by Shropshire Education Committee.

During break times, games like hopscotch, tick and kiss-chase were very popular, even if the headteacher's plimsole beckoned when things got out of hand. Christmas was invariably celebrated with a ativity play and party, where jelly and ice cream were washed down with lashings of weak orange squash before re-entering the world during subsequent energetic games.

Eleven-plus examinations for ten and eleven-year-olds were greeted with immeasurable trepidation by both children and parents alike, so much depended on the outcome. Equating success with social class (or aspiration) is naïve in the extreme, yet the pressures to pass examinations placed on children by teachers, let alone parents, were immense.

To fail was much worse than fainting in the queue for vaccinations against polio or squirming under the nit-nurse's comb. Failure was often cruelly associated with stupidity; the Secondary Modern school in 1960 was still suffering from the perception that it was academically lacking, although in technical subjects it was one of the best in the district. Nevertheless, some children would rather be 'grammar grubs' than 'modern monkeys'. Many tears were shed over eleven-plus results.

Children's achievements should not be measured solely by paper qualifications, but it was partly because of prevailing attitudes (held by many 'educationalists' and employers) that the Certificate of Secondary Education (CSE) examinations were designed specifically for secondary modern schools. Everyone knew that the standards set were lower than the General Certificate Examinations (GCEs, known as 'O', 'A' and 'S' levels) taken by grammar- and high-

Prince's Street Junior School children at their Christmas party.

Park Junior School staged a seventeenth-century May celebration to commemorate the tercentenary of King Charles II's return from exile in 1660. Prominence was, of course, given to the famous Royal Oak, here made with a climbing frame and hula hoops, with a few authentic twigs. From left to right, back row: Jane Gale, Allan Frost, Howard Bowen, John Fifield, Sally ?, -?-, Jane Lawton, Richard Young, Julie Leighton, -?-, David Weston, -?-, Andrew White. Middle row: Laurel Cooke, Alan Reeve, Paul James. Front row: Celia West (?), -?-, Janice ?, Marilyn Jones (?), Diane Meakin, Linda Yarnold.

Park Junior School handicrafts competition, October 1960. The exhibitors pictured here are Christine Burden, Christine Chesters, Hilary Bale, Hilary Rainford, Gareth Goodwin, Helen Rawlins, Stephen Addison, Peter Overton and Keith Horton.

school pupils but at least children were able to present a certificate to prospective employers.

Children progressing to one of the secondary schools would go, with their parents, to an evening meeting where they were told more about the school's facilities and culture. They would also be expected to buy essential items like sports kit and uniforms; some things, including outdated caps, were available secondhand from older pupils who had outgrown still-serviceable garments. Grammar school boys were also expected to pay sixpence for a copy of the school rules, which were quite comprehensive and, unfortunately, showed parents how much time should be spent on homework each night.

Some form of ability-streaming took place in all junior and secondary schools (as did the system of prefects to enforce discipline); as with the eleven-plus, once teachers had decided a child's ability (often with limited evidence), it was almost impossible to relocate to a more appropriate stream. Teachers did not seem to like their judgement or performance coming under scrutiny or their authority being questioned, which was probably why a few appeared to relish excessive sarcasm and even resorted to acts of mild brutality. The same situation arose when pupils made choices on which subjects to study for their GCEs; teachers (or 'masters' and 'mistresses' as they were called at the grammar and high schools) were sometimes known to influence decisions adversely.

Notwithstanding weaknesses in the educational system, Wellington schools served their pupils well and many made remarkable achievements in their academic, sporting and social endeavours. There can be very few who resented what were, in many respects, the best years of their lives. It is surprising how many teachers' nicknames (Sheriff, Adam, Mo, The Bogue and Snoz to name but a few from the grammar school) can be recalled with a degree of affection, even though their actual surnames or reasons for the nicknames cannot.

A section of the 1960 official photograph of pupils and teachers at Orleton Lane Secondary Modern School. The headmaster was Alfred Shimeld. Building work was soon to begin on a new girls' modern school at Dothill (Charlton School) which would separate the sexes. The boys would remain at Orleton Lane.

Park Junior School's modern dance entry at the Shropshire Schools Dancing Festival, November 1960. From left to right, back row: Edward Roderick, Allan Frost, Andrew White, -?-, Alan Reeve, -?-, Paul James, -?-. Second row from back: Christine Faulkner (?), Sandra Guest, Linda Yarnold, Jane Gale, Christrine Rubery, Margot Hewlett, -?-, Amanda Smith, Gillian Howells. Second row from front: Janice ?, Gwen Crittenden, Stella Tinsley. Front row: Joanne Harper, -?-, Hilary Bale, Hilary Rainford, Geraldine Price, Sally ?, Lesley Onions, Laurel Cooke.

Girls High School prefects, 1959/60. From left to right, back row: I. Cadman, M. Brown, P. Brayne. Middle row: W. Clifford, P. Abbott, A. Shimeld, S. Pearce, R. Evason, D. Evans, P. Small, P. Wynn Green. Front row: K. Giles, E. Aspey, J. Stordy, Miss Ethel Barnes (headmistress), J. Swift, J. Pardoe, S. Griffiths.

F. ABSENCE.

1. No boy may be absent from School except for ill-health or other urgent reason unless permission has previously been obtained from the Head Master. Such permission should be sought by note from parent or guardian.

2. On returning after absence from School, a boy must bring a note to his Form Master from his parent or guardian stating the cause and duration of absence.

3. Parents are asked to inform the Head Master as early as possible when a boy has contracted an infectious disease or is in quarantine because of contact with an infectious disease. In such cases, boys must bring a note certifying freedom from infection on their return to School

G. SCHOOL DINNERS.

1. Boys may take dinner at School if they wish but if they intend to do so notice must be given at the beginning of each term, and those who give such notice are expected to take dinner each day. Where a boy has stated that he will be taking School dinner a note from his parent is required if for special reasons he wishes not to take dinner on a particular day. Casual attendance at dinner is not permitted.

2. Boys not going home to dinner may, if they do not wish to take School dinner, be permitted (if their parents so desire) to take dinner in the town. In such cases parents should state, in a note to the Head Master, the place where their boy will be having dinner. This should be done at the beginning of each term, and the Head Master should be notified in writing of any variation.

3. Boys bringing packed food to School for mid-day meals will eat it in the Dining Hall. All boys having meals in the Hall are expected to observe proper table manners, good order and consideration for others.

H. MISCELLANEOUS.

1. Eating is not allowed on the School premises during class-room hours, or at any other time in any of the School Buildings except the Hall.

2. No boy is to walk about within the School Buildings eating ice-cream, fruit, cake or similar food.

3. Boys should not eat in the streets, or any public place such as a bus or station platform, whether it is a question of sweets, chewing-gum or ice-cream. This, like the combing of hair in public, is an offence against good manners .

4. No boy is to smoke or have material for smoking in his possession on the School premises, nor may he smoke in public while wearing School uniform. Any smoking at all during a boy's school career not only undesirable but ill-advised in his own interest.

5. No boy is to be in possession of or to use any explosive substance, air-pistol, water-pistol, catapult, peashooter or any other dangerous contrivance on tne School premises.

6. All accidents on the School premises must be reported to a Master immediately. Rollers and mowing machines are a particular source of danger. Boys must not use the former except under supervision ; the latter must not be used by boys in any case.

7. Detention takes place on Wednesday and Friday and may take place on other days when necessary. A clear day's notice is given to boys required to attend, so that parents may be informed of the reason for late return from School. Detention takes precedence of all other activities. Requests for special dispensation must be made to the Second Master, and absence without such permission is regarded as a very serious offence.

8. Activities advertised on the School Calendar Board and Card take precedence of all others except detention.

9. Out-of School activities are normally voluntary, but once a boy has joined some voluntary activity acts of misconduct or lack of consideration affecting that activity may be treated as normal School offences

10. It is an offence to leave money or other valuables in cloak-rooms or desks.

11. All illustrated magazines, papers or ' comics ' are liable to confiscation if brought into class-rooms.

12. **General.** (a) Boys are reminded that the good name of the School depends on their individual conduct wherever they may be. The School authorities therefore take cognisance of such conduct and will deal with offences against the principles of behaviour laid down at School even though these offences may take place away from the School premises, in particular on public conveyances.

Among the more serious offences are bullying, hooliganism and the use of bad language. Conduct of this sort, whether committed on or off the School premises is a serious reflection on the School and will be dealt with severely.

An extract from the Boys Grammar School book of school rules.

Boys Grammar School prefects, 1960/61. From left to right, back row: R.W. Lambert, R.H. Harris, A.J. Poole, I.R. Edwards, D. Russon, H.J. Pickering, J.R. Hassall, A.R. Jones. Middle row: A.G.R.C. Knipe, R.N. Briscoe, A. West, G.R. Gittins, E.C. Farthing, P.E. Marchetti, C.P. Power, B. Earle. Front row: K.B. Edwards, M.R. Corfield, D.L. Frost (school captain), John Llewellyn Morgan-Jones (headmaster), J. Johnson, G.I. Holloway, W.C. Newbold.

To many people, Sunday school education was an important aspect of a child's upbringing, with children often attending school at both morning and afternoon sessions. Methodists held Sunday school anniversaries in very high regard – not only did they promote the learning of new hymns and recitations but also provided an enjoyable form of religious entertainment. Here, Tan Bank Methodist Sunday School children, supported by their teachers and members of the church choir, appear at the anniversary held in May 1960. From left to right, back row: Eustace Mosdell, Ken Sands, Bob Pritchard, Len Boughey, George Evans. Seventh row: Nell Harding, Emily Boughey, Dorothy Mosdell, Pauline Sands, Irene Eccleshall, Margaret Bellingham, Diane Boughey, Sheila Bardsley. Sixth row: Mary Bengry, Dorothy Waters (?), Margaret Rhodes, Elsie Sands, Milly McCleod, Wyn Morris, Janet Morris, Sylvia Johnson. Fifth row includes Frances Jones, Tania Price, Jennifer Brown. Fourth row: Davina Johnson. Third row: Sheila Whittaker, Iris Johnson, Tina Price. Second row: Jane Phillips, Sue Jackson, Gillian Price. Front row: Rosemary Ward.

Fifteen

1960 Diary

JANUARY: A séance was held to lay to rest the disturbed soul of Humphrey, resident ghost at the Swan Inn, Watling Street. One of the oldest buildings in Wellington, dating back to c. 1416, the ancient timbers finally succumbed to the silent ravages of woodworm and deathwatch beetle. Landlord John Wilson (who also owned Buckatree Hall) acceded to the wishes of his staff to release Humphrey from his earthly bondage before the building was demolished. Messrs Butler & Co., brewers of Wolverhampton, later built a new public house on the site; this was to open in November.

Charlton Hall (formerly and still known as the town hall) in Market Street was refurbished. Staff from the Wrekin Brewery and O.D. Murphy's pop works were the first to hold a dinner dance there when it reopened.

R.G. Murphy denied reports that Marks & Spencer had made a bid to buy the Duke of Wellington public house in High Street from the Wrekin Brewery.

Vineyard Children's Home performed a nativity play produced by its superintendent Mr C.F. Jones.

Cheryl Griffiths, Sarah Hutchins, Judith Ralph and Andrea Peplow were some of the children who won fancy-dress competitions at the Post Office staff children's party in the Majestic ballroom.

'New contemporary type' houses at Brooklands, off North Road, were advertised for £1875. They were erected by Fletcher Estates of Shrewsbury.

Victor George Leake, joint managing director of the *Wellington Journal & Shrewsbury News*, died aged seventy-two. He was the grandson of Thomas Leake, who had founded the *Journal* in 1854.

Mrs Martha Amelia Bentley, one of the joint founders of Wellington Laundry (at Belle Vue Cottages, Prince's Street, in 1893), died at the Priory Nursing Home, aged ninety-three. She and her husband William began the business in a corrugated iron shed.

222 birds took part in the Shropshire Caged Birds Society show at Belmont Hall.

Wellington Townswomen's Guild held its annual dinner at the Charlton Arms Hotel. Members of the Guild's drama group (Fifi Cooper-Edmonds, M. Balderstone, A. Whittle, P. Hewitson, J. Leighton and I. Stafford) provided entertainment.

British Road Services, whose large depot was located on the corner of Watling Street and Arleston Lane, held its annual dinner for its employees at the Forest Glen. Safe driving awards were presented to worthy drivers.

The old Roman Catholic school on Mill Bank was in such a deplorable state that a new secondary school for the older pupils still attending (juniors were catered for at their own school in North Road) was scheduled to be built in 1961-62 elsewhere in the town. Blessed Robert Johnson Catholic College was the result.

Bernard Bagnall produced *It's a Wonderful Life*, the seventh biannual Gang Show performed by the 2nd Wellington Scout Group at Wellington Youth Centre, Constitution Hill.

Dr Barbara Moore (aged fifty-six) walked through the town, spending a night at the Charlton Arms Hotel, on her landmark journey from John O'Groats to Lands End.

1960 was the centenary year of the Chad Valley Company (named after the Chad, a small stream at Harborne, Birmingham, where the company's head office moved in 1897). Their Wrekin Toy Works, located in the former Wesleyan Methodist chapel, New Street, was opened in the early 1920s. (For more information, see *The Chad Valley Wrekin Toy Works and Noah Frost's Bakery Row* by the same author.)

Thieves smashed windows at the Radio & Television Repair shop in Walker Street and E.W. Jones Electrical in New Street. Radios and televisions were stolen.

Heavy snow fell throughout the county, causing considerable disruption to traffic and life generally. The cold spell continued until mid-February.

FEBRUARY: Wrekin Labour Party held a public meeting in Morris Hall, calling for a boycott of South African goods in protest against racial discrimination.

Wellington Road Safety Committee reported that there were fifty-two accidents between the Cock Hotel and the Buck's Head public house during 1959.

Mr. J.A. Smith decided he would retire shortly and sell his fishmonger's premises at 65 New Street. It became Ming Fung, the first Chinese restaurant in the town, later in the year.

All Saints Parish church clock acted very strangely; it had a fit of striking incorrectly and did not keep time. A maintenance mechanic had left a spanner in the works.

Toc H society headquarters had to leave to be relocated from its rented room in Station Approach and moved temporarily into Belmont Hall.

Revd Peter A. Tubbs was appointed curate of Christ Church.

The Buckatree Hall Hotel Club was granted a license to sell intoxicating liquor. Owner John Wilson was pleased; he had acquired the hall in May 1959 to develop it into a first class hotel.

The Ten Commandments was shown at the Clifton cinema for an exceptional ten days. Upstairs circle seats cost 5s. The manager, Ray Lifton-Head, had to apologize when the projector failed several times during a Saturday afternoon matinee performance.

A puppet made by fourteen-year-old John Giles of New Street won first prize in the junior section of the British Puppet and Model Theatre Guild Exhibition. By this time he had made some fifty-six puppets, mainly from clay and papier-mache, although the winning entry was hand-carved from wood.

Adults under forty years old were advised to be vaccinated against poliomyelitis.

MARCH: Licensing Justices for the Wrekin area banned the use of jukeboxes in public houses because of the annoyance they caused to regulars.

Levi Thomas Jarman of Vineyard Road died aged eighty-three. He had been a chimney sweep for over sixty years and had bought his first car in 1910.

Miss Isobel Gwynne was chosen as Miss Wellington Wrekin Conservative.

APRIL: Wellington Rural District Council tenants were in for a shocking rent increase of 1s 11d. The revised weekly rent became 14s 3d.

Minister of Education Sir David Eccles stated that work on the new Walker Technical College at Bennett's Bank (begun in July 1959) should be completed by August 1961. The college would be formally opened in November 1962.

Herbert Peake retired from his employment with timber merchants R. Groom & Sons after fifty-seven years service.

The Charlton Arms Hotel opened its new Steak House bar. The manager then was Mr V.T. Walker.

A baby elephant walked from the railway station to a field belonging to Barnfield Farm, Haygate (next to Oaks Crescent), to advertise a visit from Robert Bros Circus and Zoo.

Mr Y. Loginov, a secretary to the USSR embassy, spoke at the Rotary International rally at the Forest Glen. He told visitors that as well as having their photographs published in local newspapers, hooligans in Russia were made to do menial work like sweeping the streets.

William Edward Steventon, tailor and gentleman's outfitter at his shop in Church Street for over thirty-nine years, died. He had taken over Richard Brisbourne's business on returning to civilian life after the First World War.

MAY: Miss B.K. Absolon replaced Miss F. M. Pye as headmistress of Orleton Lane County Infants School.

250 men of the King's Shropshire Light Infantry 1st Battalion paraded through the town, led, at their nippy regulation pace, by their band. The visit was part of the battalion's 'getting to know you' route march through many of Shropshire's towns and villages. The tour culminated in a gymnastics and weaponry display held on the car park on what is now The Parade.

John Llewellyn Morgan-Jones, headmaster of Wellington Grammar School, appeared as a witness when a van driver was prosecuted for reversing into a car parked outside Lloyds Bank.

Stan Price from Ludlow won Wrekin Golf Club's Spring Open with a score of sixty-seven, equaling a long-standing record. Par for the course was sixty-nine.

Mrs Agnes Mary Jones of Ercall Lane became the first woman chair of the Urban District Council. She succeeded Philip Bott whose last duty had been to have lunch with the mayor of Wellington, South Africa, who happened to be passing through the town at the time.

Albert Gates, the last of Wellington's coal

merchants to deliver with a horse and dray, died aged seventy-five after retiring five years earlier.

The Boys' Grammar School annual sports day took place. Trophy winners were Ray Gittins, Roy Mack, Michael Bolderstone, Robert Lambert, David Pointon and M. Hughes. Wrekin House came first, Ercall second and Lawrence third.

Chetwoods opened a new petrol filling station in Foundry Road.

JUNE: E.W. Jones Electrical purchased Norah Wellings' Victoria Toy factory in King Street with a view to centralizing the company's operations. Unfortunately, Mr Jones died later in the year.

Shropshire roads were reported as being the worst in the country.

Charlton Arms Bowling Club celebrated its 100th anniversary. Originally, its green was near the Market Hall, then moved to behind the old Bull's Head Hotel in New Street before settling at its current location. In the early days, boys were employed to pick up the bowls so that members wearing silk hats and Wellington boots, did not have to stoop down.

Eight acres of gorse and woodland caught fire on the Wrekin Hill.

Wellington & District Sportsmen's Committee Whit Saturday Carnival (to give it its proper name) made a record profit of £785. A donation to the British Empire Cancer Campaign, to 'help research scientists find the answer to a baffling problem', was made later in the year. Camilla Yates, wife of the Wrekin MP, crowned Carnival Queen Miss Daphne Holland after the procession through the streets terminated at the Buck's Head football ground. Wrekin Hospital's tableau came second in the Best Decorated (non-advertising) class while Wellington Swimming Club came third; The Chad Valley Company came first in the Best Decorated (advertising) class. Jacqueline Spicer won the under-six-months Beautiful Baby competition. Bands and dance troops entertained the crowd. The carnival was sponsored by the *Wellington Journal & Shrewsbury News*.

Wellington Urban District Council considered allowing their employees to work a five day week.

A *Journal* reporter noted that car aerials were becoming more common as increasing numbers of drivers wanted to listen to music while driving. Some cars had two aerials to improve reception.

New Street Methodist Sunday school anniversary was held.

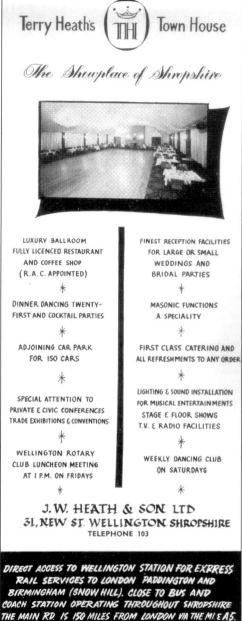

Terry Heath's TH **Town House**

The Showplace of Shropshire

LUXURY BALLROOM FULLY LICENCED RESTAURANT AND COFFEE SHOP (R.A.C. APPOINTED)

FINEST RECEPTION FACILITIES FOR LARGE OR SMALL WEDDINGS AND BRIDAL PARTIES

DINNER DANCING TWENTY-FIRST AND COCKTAIL PARTIES

MASONIC FUNCTIONS A SPECIALITY

ADJOINING CAR PARK FOR 150 CARS

FIRST CLASS CATERING AND ALL REFRESHMENTS TO ANY ORDER

SPECIAL ATTENTION TO PRIVATE & CIVIC CONFERENCES TRADE EXHIBITIONS & CONVENTIONS

LIGHTING & SOUND INSTALLATION FOR MUSICAL ENTERTAINMENTS STAGE & FLOOR SHOWS T.V. & RADIO FACILITIES

WELLINGTON ROTARY CLUB LUNCHEON MEETING AT 1 P.M. ON FRIDAYS

WEEKLY DANCING CLUB ON SATURDAYS

J. W. HEATH & SON LTD 31, NEW ST. WELLINGTON SHROPSHIRE TELEPHONE 103

DIRECT ACCESS TO WELLINGTON STATION FOR EXPRESS RAIL SERVICES TO LONDON PADDINGTON AND BIRMINGHAM (SNOW HILL). CLOSE TO BUS AND COACH STATION OPERATING THROUGHOUT SHROPSHIRE THE MAIN RD. IS 150 MILES FROM LONDON VIA THE M1 & A5.

Terry Heath's Town House, 'The Showplace of Shropshire', was officially opened in June by Terry's wife Mary, with many invited personalities dancing to music played by Frank Clayton and his Orchestra. The hall cost over £25,000 and became a venue for Saturday dances and dinners for countless organizations.

About 450 swimmers regularly attended Wellington Baths every Saturday. The council couldn't make up its mind about whether to build a new pool at Dothill or to extend, or rebuild, the existing baths. It would be twenty more years before the old baths were replaced.

JULY: Work began on an automatic telephone exchange in Haygate Road. When completed, subscribers would be able to dial, for example, London direct for only 2d per call.

Miss Valerie Goodger of Albrighton was selected Wrekin Labour Queen at a dance held at Terry Heath's town house. She was given her sash by Daphne Barber, the retiring Queen.

Wellington Girls High School pupil Wendy Hancox received an invitation to visit Buckingham Palace to see the Queen. Her father, Mr T.C. Hancox, had been a member of the 3rd Battalion Grenadier Guards, which was about to be merged with the 2nd Battalion. The Queen invited representatives to the Palace to express her gratitude for the Battalion's past service. Mr Hancox was well known locally for his interest in the history of Wellington.

Wellington Library opened its musical record collection. Plans to extend the library 'within the next year' were confirmed, which would enable the Children's Library annexe to be incorporated into the main building.

Inverness was the furthest destination reached by a balloon from the race launched at the Whit Saturday Carnival. Patricia Wilde of Donnington was the winner.

Secondary modern girls staged a mannequin parade as part of the school's open day.

Ron Lewin, manager of the town's football team, commented on the nature of supporters: during the week, he said, they are hen-pecked and daren't say a word at home. But on Saturday they pour abuse over twenty-two men as hard as they can! Club president J.T. Stone said, 'I do think the gates are shocking at Wellington. I don't know what we'd do without the supporters' club. It is bad for a place like Wellington, with houses going up and increases in population, to have gates like these'.

The new road between New Street and the railway station was due to be called Central Road, but the council changed its mind and called it The Parade.

AUGUST: An American satellite was spotted in the night sky over the Wrekin Hill.

Dr I.E. Davidson moved house from Church Street into one on the corner of Crescent Road and Vineyard Road. Thereafter he was plagued by a mystery doorbell ringer until the *Journal* appealed for the miscreant to stop.

Danish Scouts returned home after a two week exchange visit to Wellington. A prominent member of the town chatted to one of the Scout leaders and commented on how good his English was, even down to the local dialect. He was, of course, speaking to one of the Wellington troops' leaders, not a Dane!

The fire brigade rescued a seventeen-year-old sailor, home on leave, who was trying to climb up the cliff of the disused quarry next to the Forest Glen.

One of the YMCA's Junior Boys' Club train-spotters (who had recently 'copped' over 200 engines in a day) was sent to Coventry by other members for breaking union rules. Apparently he went on holiday with his parents in a car, not by rail!

John Scott of 64 High Street discovered a rare queen hornet with a half-inch sting in his wash-house.

Miss Celia Godbert was appointed headmistress of Constitution Hill Infants School, having previously been deputy head at Barn Farm School. Her retiring predecessor was Miss M.L. Evans.

Dawley residents noted a substantial number of aircraft flying at low levels and apparently taking aerial photographs. A *Journal* report linked the observation to suspected Ministry of Housing plans to build a new town to cater for some 6,000 of Birmingham's 'overspill' population. Mr C. Savage, surveyor to Dawley Urban District Council, said, 'We have received no official information of any large-scale development as suggested by reports'. The report is of no concern to inhabitants of Wellington. Or Oakengates. Or Madeley. Or Ironbridge. It wouldn't affect them…

SEPTEMBER: Over 120 pieces of medieval pottery were found by student archaeologists from Sheffield University while excavating at Dothill prior to the commencement of new building work. The shards indicated that a dwelling of some sort was occupied there between AD 1150 and at least 1300, but no later than the Tudor period.

Miss Edith Picton-Turberville, the first woman Member of Parliament when elected Labour representative for the Wrekin constituency in 1929, died aged eighty-eight at her home in Cheltenham. During her two years as an MP she successfully introduced a bill to prevent expectant mothers from receiving the death penalty.

On 12 September, Ministry of Transport (MOT) tests were introduced, to be carried out on all cars over ten years old. Many local garages were appointed as authorized examination centers.

OCTOBER: Mr G.H. Bond retired after over thirty-six years as registrar, during which time he recorded 16,000 births and 9,000 deaths. Mr A.E. Gaut succeeded him.

Rose Podmore died aged sixty-eight. She had once been licensee of the Nelson Inn in High Street – a position she held for over twenty years.

Building work began on a new Esso petrol station on the corner of Walker Street and Wrekin Road. Bernard Bagnall, of Boy Scouting and Wellington Town Football Club fame, would be its occupier.

Ernest William Jones died, aged eighty, at his home at 21 Waterloo Road. His electrical business had begun during the early 1920s and he had been chairman of the town's football team for several years after 1953.

After a vacancy lasting some three years, Revd Edwin H. Newton took up the post of pastor at Union Free church.

The *Journal* reported that the art of navigation temporarily escaped six Wellington Sea Rangers who were on their way to appear in a variety performance at Donnington Methodist church. They lost their way amid a dark and stormy night. The group tried three churches before heading back home. They got back safely.

NOVEMBER: MP Bill Yates said the Wrekin constituency would welcome the Minster for Housing's New Town in the Wrekin area and considered it a good use of land. 'The whole county will welcome this town', he added.

A crowded meeting of Wellington Licensed Victuallers Association strongly disagreed with a Parliamentary bill to extend Sunday lunchtime opening hours by one hour. The extension was described as absurd and totally unnecessary.

Ambitious plans for housing and amenities at Dothill were revealed by the Urban District Council. In fact, the plans were a little too ambitious, and expected cricket and other sports pitches, tennis courts, bowling rink and putting green failed to materialize. A new secondary modern school for girls and blocks of flats were to appear during the course of the next few years, as was more housing – rates bring in money, sporting facilities do not.

Residents on the new Dothill and Brooklands estates were up in arms against having to use smokeless fuel, which was more expensive, when their neighbours in North Road were able to burn ordinary coal. Councillor Tom Edwards said, 'We have got to start somewhere and we hope eventually to have all smokeless zones in the area'.

Two men were arrested for acts of gross indecency after a policeman spied on them through a hole in the wall at New Street car park toilets.

Wellington Theatre Club performed a comedy at the Drill Hall. Among the cast were Fifi Cooper-Edmonds and Ceri Griffiths. The producer was Jose Grant, a hairdresser in New Street.

DECEMBER: Methane gas was pumped from Granville Colliery at Donnington Wood to Wellington Gas Works, and mixed with 'town gas' before being supplied to households. Unlike North Sea gas, the highly toxic town gas had a distinctive smell and was the cause of several head-in-the-oven and unlit-gas-fire suicides during the year.

Sheila Moore won the title of Mistletoe Queen 1960 at the seventh annual Mistletoe Ball held in the Drill Hall, King Street.

Walter Davies, formerly an outfitter in the town who had operated from premises in Market Square since 1905, died aged eighty-six.

War was declared by L.J. Holbrook, chairman of the Shropshire branch of the National Farmers Union, on rabbits, as well as on landowners who refused to take action to reduce their numbers.

The post office enlisted help from older pupils at the high and grammar schools to cope with the Christmas mail. The girls worked in the sorting office and the boys took deliveries.

Fireman R. Mitchell rescued a fourteen-year-old boy from a rock face behind the Forest Glen Pavilion.

Council chairman Agnes Jones visited inmates at Wrekin Hospital on Christmas Day. Four children were born at the hospital that day. The mothers were Eileen Jenkins, who gave birth to a daughter, and Christine Cartledge, Rosemary Skeet and Mary Wilcox, who all had sons.

Get the Picture?

Such a book as this would not have been possible without the remarkable photographs taken by Bernard Cross and his employees Sheila Howard, Colin Bebb and Godfrey Evans. In the author's opinion, they will prove to be as historically important as the relatively few and fairly select photographs produced as postcards by companies such as Frith and Valentine. 1960 was something of a watershed in Wellington's history; anyone that had visited the centre of the town in 1910 and returned in 1960 would recognize many familiar sights. Since then there have been many changes, not just in the town's appearance but also in the way Wellingtonians live.

Copies, including enlargements, of the 133 photographs credited 'copyright Abbeycolor' in this book, together with almost 200 more, can be obtained from Art Etc, the company's agents for their photographs relating specifically to Wellington.

Art Etc can be contacted at their shop at 12 Duke Street, Wellington, Telford, Shropshire TF1 1BJ, England, telephone 01952 257611. Their web site is www.wrekinarts.co.uk and emails can be sent to artetc@wrekinarts.co.uk.

The Wrekin Hill beacon, apparently installed around 1943 to warn aircraft away from the hill's summit, was viewed with a great deal of affection by local residents. Waving goodnight to the flashing red light became a bedtime ritual for many children. It also gave a feeling of relief when returning from tedious coach journeys – if the light could be seen, home was not far away. Despite public appeals and questions raised in Parliament, the beacon was eventually dismantled in August 1970 and probably scrapped, although rumours persist that it was taken to Australia.